THE OLD
FARMER'S ALMANAC

FOR

VOLUME 8

YANKEE PUBLISHING INCORPORATED

The Old Farmer's Almanac Books

Publisher: Sherin Pierce
Editor in chief: Janice Stillman
Art director: Colleen Quinnell
Series editor: Sarah Perreault
Managing editor: Jack Burnett
Contributors: Quinten Albrecht, Carol Mowdy Bond, Christopher Burnett, Jack Burnett, Alice Cary, Melissa Caughey, Tim Clark, Stephanie Gibeault, Brenda Huante, Mare-Anne Jarvela, Benjamin Kilbride, Barbara Lassonde, Sheryl Normandeau, Sarah Perreault, Stephanie Shaw, Janice Stillman, Heidi Stonehill

V.P., New Media and production: Paul Belliveau
Production directors: Susan Gross, David Ziarnowski
Production artists: Jennifer Freeman, Janet Selle, Susan Shute

Companion Web site: Almanac4kids.com

Digital editor: Catherine Boeckmann
Assistant digital editor: Christopher Burnett
New Media designers: Lucio S. Eastman, Amy O'Brien
E-commerce manager: Alan Henning
Programming: Reinvented, Inc.

For additional information about this and other publications from *The Old Farmer's Almanac,* visit **Almanac.com** or call **877-717-8924**

Distributed in the book trade in the United States by Houghton Mifflin Harcourt and in Canada by Thomas Allen & Son Limited

Direct-to-retail and bulk sales are handled by Stacey Korpi, 800-895-9265, ext. 160

Yankee Publishing Inc., P.O. Box 520, 1121 Main Street, Dublin, New Hampshire 03444

ISBN: 978-1-57198-817-1

ISSN: 1948-061X

FIRST PRINTING OF VOLUME 8

Thank you to everyone who had a hand in producing this Almanac and getting it to market, including printers, distributors, and sales and delivery people, and thanks to all of you who bought it!

HEY, KIDS!

Here we—and you—go again!
Welcome to the newest edition of
The Old Farmer's Almanac for Kids!

You'll get many hours of fun from this book . . .

- Share it with your family and friends
- Try the activities
- Cook the recipes
- Tell the riddles
- Grow in the garden
- Play the games
- Get inspired by kids just like you
- Learn a gazillion interesting facts!

Whether this is your first *Old Farmer's Almanac for Kids* or your 8th, you have a fascinating reading adventure ahead!

We'd love to hear what you think about this book. Send us your thoughts, opinions, ideas, and impressions at **Almanac.com/feedback** or mail a letter to **The Old Farmer's Almanac for Kids, P.O. Box 520, Dublin, NH 03444.**

From each and every one of us to each and every one of you, turn the page and have fun!

–The Almanac Editors

CONTENTS

FAMILY TREE

8

36

40

56

ON THE FARM

IN THE GARDEN

NATURE

CONTENTS

124

148

158

140

HEALTH

PETS

AMUSEMENT

We know that some months have unique reasons for celebration—
think May (Mother's Day), June (Father's Day), October (Halloween),
December (Christmas and Kwanzaa). But **every month is special!**
Here are some events and observations to note throughout the year.

JANUARY

JANUARY HAS 31 DAYS.

The first month is named for the Roman god Janus, protector of gates and doorways. Janus has two faces, one looking to the past and the other to the future.

January's **FULL WOLF MOON** was named for wolves, which tended to howl more often at this time.

AS THE DAY LENGTHENS, SO THE COLD STRENGTHENS.

SKY HIGHS

Every year, at its perihelion in the first week of January, Earth is closest to the Sun, approximately 91,402,000 miles away.

CARNATION

BIRTHSTONE: GARNET

Garnet is usually red. It was often a good luck charm, keeping the wearer safe during travel.

BIRTH FLOWERS: CARNATION AND SNOWDROP

Red carnation means "I love you," while snowdrop signifies hope.

JANUARY 1, 1892

The first immigrant to pass through Ellis Island into the United States was 15-year-old Annie Moore, from Ireland.

JANUARY 9, 1996

The NBA's Toronto Raptors became the first professional basketball team to miss all of its free throw attempts in a game.

JANUARY 13

In Sweden, this is the traditional day to discard the Christmas tree and end the season's festivities by "dancing" the tree out the door while singing.

JANUARY 14, 2011

A rare black rhinoceros was born at Missouri's St. Louis Zoo.

JANUARY 19

NATIONAL POPCORN DAY
Before serving, put just-cooked popcorn into a large bag with a small hole cut in the bottom, then shake. The "old maids"—unpopped kernels—will fall out.

JANUARY 18, 1882

Birth date of *Winnie the Pooh* writer A. A. Milne

February

WINTER'S BACK BREAKS ABOUT THE MIDDLE OF FEBRUARY.

FEBRUARY HAS 28 DAYS— UNTIL LEAP YEAR, WHEN IT HAS ONE MORE.

The second month gets its name from the Latin word *februa*, which means "to cleanse." The Roman calendar month of Februarius was named for Februalia, a festival of purification that took place during this period.

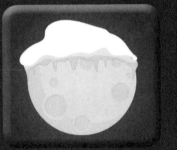

Native Americans noticed that usually the heaviest snows fall in February and named the FULL SNOW MOON for them. (For some tribes, hunting became difficult, so they called it the Hunger Moon.)

BIRTHSTONE: AMETHYST
A form of quartz, this purple stone was thought to help its wearer to think.

BIRTH FLOWERS: VIOLET AND PRIMROSE
Violet symbolizes loyalty. Primrose, when given to a friend, says, "I can not live without you."

PRIMROSE

SKY HIGHS

To keep up with Earth's orbit around the Sun and keep the four seasons on track, we add an extra day—Leap Day—to the calendar about every 4 years. This day, February 29, occurs only in years that are divisible by 4, but if the year ends in "00," it must also be divisible by 400.

FEBRUARY 2

GROUNDHOG DAY
If the Sun shines and the groundhog sees its shadow, expect 6 more weeks of winter; if there is no Sun, expect warmth and rain instead of cold and snow.

FEBRUARY 14

VALENTINE'S DAY
In Latin America, today is called the Day of Love and Friendship. It is celebrated with acts of appreciation for friends and family.

FEBRUARY 15, 1965

The current Canadian flag, designed by George Stanley, was first raised over Parliament Hill in Ottawa, Ontario.

FEBRUARY 21, 1918

The last Carolina parakeet, the only parakeet species native to the eastern U.S., died in captivity at the Cincinnati Zoo.

THIRD SATURDAY

WORLD PANGOLIN DAY
Learn about this endangered scaly anteater found in Africa and Asia—how they eat (they have no teeth!), what they eat (70 million ants a year!), and why they have their own app (Roll with the Pangolins).

MONTH'S END

INTERNATIONAL HAIR FREEZING CONTEST
At the Takhini Hot Springs in Yukon, Canada, contestants get into the springs, dunk their head into the 104°F water, push wet hair (eyebrows, mustaches, and beards) into shape before it freezes, and then take a photo after it does. The ideal air temperature for this is −4°F or colder.

MARCH

FOGS IN MARCH, FROSTS IN MAY.

MARCH HAS 31 DAYS.

March is named for the Roman god of war, Mars. Military campaigns that were interrupted by winter weather resumed at this time of year.

As the ground begins to thaw and soften, earthworm casts (poop) reappear, so Native Americans called this the **FULL WORM MOON**.

BIRTHSTONE: AQUAMARINE

Ancient sailors believed that this blue stone protected them against ocean dangers.

BIRTH FLOWERS: DAFFODIL AND JONQUIL

Daffodil signifies love, while jonquil means "please tell me that you love me, too."

DAFFODIL

SKY HIGHS

In the Northern Hemisphere, spring arrives on March 20 or 21, when the Sun crosses the celestial equator on its way north. This is called the vernal equinox.

Daylight Saving Time begins on this month's second Sunday at 2:00 A.M. Set clocks 1 hour ahead ("spring forward"), if your area observes it.

MARCH 1

In Switzerland, young boys in traditional costume parade through town ringing bells to drive out winter and welcome spring. The event was brought to life in the book *A Bell for Ursli*.

MARCH 17

It is tradition to plant peas today.

MARCH 15

This is known as Buzzard Day in Hinckley, Ohio, because turkey vultures (called buzzards) return north for food.

SECOND SATURDAY

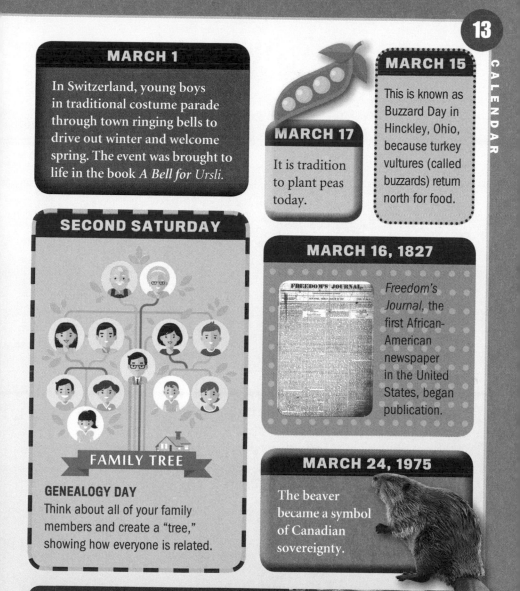

FAMILY TREE

GENEALOGY DAY

Think about all of your family members and create a "tree," showing how everyone is related.

MARCH 16, 1827

Freedom's Journal, the first African-American newspaper in the United States, began publication.

MARCH 24, 1975

The beaver became a symbol of Canadian sovereignty.

MARCH 29, 1848

At about midnight, Niagara's Horseshoe Falls stopped flowing when ice fields from Lake Erie became lodged at the mouth of the Niagara River. The ice broke up 30 hours later, freeing the water.

APRIL

APRIL HAS 30 DAYS.
The fourth month gets its name from the Latin word *aperio*, "to open (bud)," because plants begin to grow in this month.

At this time of year, Native Americans noticed blooms on moss pinks (also known as wild ground phlox), one of the first spring flowers. This is why this full Moon is named the **FULL PINK MOON.**

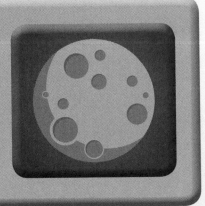

APRIL WEATHER, RAIN AND SUNSHINE, BOTH TOGETHER.

SKY HIGHS
You don't have to go to the Moon to know how much you would weigh there: Just multiply your weight (pounds or kilograms) by 0.165. You'd weigh about one-sixth as much as on Earth!

DAISY

BIRTHSTONE: DIAMOND
Made of carbon, diamond is the hardest gemstone and can be cut only by another diamond. It was once thought to protect against poisoning.

BIRTH FLOWERS: DAISY AND SWEET PEA
Daisy means hope, and sweet pea sends a blissful message.

APRIL 1

APRIL FOOLS' DAY
When several countries switched to the Gregorian calendar in the 1580s, their New Year's Day moved from March 25 to January 1. Yet, many people still celebrated the "new" year until April 1. Some believe that this is how "April fools'" got started.

APRIL 5, 1999

An April blizzard dropped 27.2 inches of snow on St. John's, Newfoundland.

SATURDAY NEAR THE FIRST QUARTER MOON

ASTRONOMY DAY
Visit a planetarium or Astroleague.org to find an astronomy club where you can learn about the sky.

APRIL 10, 1866

The American Society for the Prevention of Cruelty to Animals (ASPCA) was founded by New Yorker Henry Bergh, after he saw a carriage driver beating his fallen horse in Russia. Do something to help animals today: Put out water for the birds, step aside to let ants pass, or pick up litter around ponds and lakes so that animals don't ingest or get tangled up in it.

Homeless.
Please
Help!

APRIL 24, 1942

Lucy Maud Montgomery died on this day. She began writing a journal at age 9, published her first poem in her teens, and wrote *Anne of Green Gables* at age 29. A good book to read!

APRIL 29, 1913

Gideon Sundback received a patent for a fastener. Folks at the B. F. Goodrich Company called it the "zipper"—as we do today.

MAY

MAY HAS 31 DAYS.
The fifth month is named for the Roman goddess Maia, who oversaw the growth of plants.

Native Americans noticed that blooms spring forth in abundance at this time of year, which inspired them to name this full Moon the FULL FLOWER MOON.

SKY HIGHS
On May 1, 1996, comet Hyakutake reached perihelion (its closest point to the Sun, 21.4 million miles). It had the longest tail ever recorded—350 million miles.

BIRTHSTONE: EMERALD
A favorite of ancient Egyptian queen Cleopatra, the emerald symbolizes rebirth.

BIRTH FLOWERS: HAWTHORN AND LILY-OF-THE-VALLEY
Hawthorn signifies hope, and lily-of-the-valley symbolizes sweetness.

HAWTHORN

LILY-OF-THE-VALLEY

A SNOWSTORM IN MAY IS WORTH A WAGONLOAD OF HAY.

MAY 1, 1884

Construction began in Chicago on the first skyscraper, a 10-story building that changed architectural thinking. It was demolished in 1931 to make way for a 42-story structure.

MAY 10, 1872

Victoria Woodhull became the first woman nominated for president of the United States. This was before women had the right to vote.

Convert to metric on p. 187

MAY 15, 1900

Rain and fish fell from the sky in Olneyville, Rhode Island. Most of them were 2 to 4 inches long.

SECOND FRIDAY

FINTASTIC FRIDAY
Help to save sharks, skates, and rays. Work with a teacher to create a program by making posters, showing films, reading, and talking about sharks. Visit an aquarium, in person or virtually.

MAY 24, 2006

When an electrical relay malfunctioned, the clock on the Peace Tower at Canada's parliament buildings in Ottawa stopped for the first time in its 25 years of telling time.

END OF MAY

CHEESE-ROLLING IN GLOUCESTERSHIRE, ENGLAND
Thousands celebrate the return of spring by watching folks chase big cheese wheels down Cooper's Hill.

JUNE

IT IS NOT SUMMER UNTIL THE CRICKETS SING.

JUNE HAS 30 DAYS.
The sixth month is named for the Roman goddess Juno, patroness of marriage.

Native American tribes knew this month's full Moon as a time to gather ripening strawberries and thus named it the **FULL STRAWBERRY MOON.**

A GOOD LEAK [RAIN] IN JUNE SETS ALL IN TUNE.

SKY HIGHS
June 20, 21, or 22 is the date of the summer solstice, when the Sun rises and sets at its northernmost points, the line known as the Tropic of Cancer; is highest in the sky at local noon, making shadows short; and gives us the "longest" day (most hours of sunlight) for the year in the Northern Hemisphere.

BIRTHSTONE: PEARL
Created when mollusks (clams, oysters, and mussels) have an irritant inside their shell, pearls symbolize purity.

BIRTH FLOWERS: HONEYSUCKLE AND ROSE
Honeysuckle symbolizes affection, while rose indicates love.

ROSE

FIRST WEDNESDAY

GLOBAL RUNNING DAY

Join millions of runners around the world! Get up and get moving: Run around the block, play tag, stage a relay. Research the Million Kid Run and work with a teacher to organize an event at your school.

JUNE 24, 2010

American John Isner defeated Nicolas Mahut of France at Wimbledon in the longest match to date— 11 hours and 5 minutes.

JOHN ISNER

JUNE 13, 1884

The world's first roller coaster opened at Coney Island, New York.

JUNE 29, 1963

Forty-four inches of snow fell on the Livingston (Alberta) Ranger Station, for the largest summer snowfall ever recorded in Canada.

LAST WEEKEND

PURPLEHULL PEA-SHELLING COMPETITION

Since 1989, this has been an event at the PurpleHull Pea Festival in Emerson, Arkansas. Contestants shell for 5 minutes, then peas are weighed. PurpleHull peas are also known as cowpeas. Research how to grow them and try it.

July

BIRTHSTONE: RUBY
Rubies (and related sapphires), are the second hardest natural gemstones. Rubies were worn by warriors for protection and symbolize love.

BIRTH FLOWERS: LARKSPUR AND WATER LILY
The larkspur indicates lightheartedness, while the water lily symbolizes purity of heart.

WATER LILY

JULY HAS 31 DAYS.
The seventh month is named to honor Roman dictator Julius Caesar (100 B.C.–44 B.C.), who helped to develop the Julian calendar, the precursor to the Gregorian calendar used today.

At this time, a buck's antlers are in full growth mode, so Native Americans named this full Moon the FULL BUCK MOON.

SKY HIGHS
In early July, Earth is at the point in its orbit that is most distant from the Sun—the aphelion—approximately 94,509,000 miles away.

JULY 1, 1980

"O, Canada" officially became the national anthem of Canada. Write an anthem for your neighborhood, school, or community that can be sung to a familiar tune.

JULY 12, 2015

Scott Jurek completed the full Appalachian Trail in 46 days, 8 hours, and 8 minutes, setting a new record by 3 hours.

JULY 14, 2015

A 75-foot pile of snow left over from winter in Boston, Massachusetts, finally completely melted.

JULY 20, 1969

Apollo 11's lunar module, *Eagle,* landed the first two humans on the Moon: commander Neil Armstrong and pilot Buzz Aldrin. They explored the Moon for 2½ hours before departing.

JULY 24, 1996

Orange-size hail fell on Calgary, Alberta.

JULY 29

GLOBAL TIGER DAY
With wild tigers endangered, scientists want to double the population by 2022. Invite friends to help host a Wild Tiger Day in your neighborhood and get kids involved in research, presentations, and games.

THUNDER AND LIGHTNING IN THE SUMMER SHOW THE POINT FROM WHICH THE FRESHENING BREEZE WILL BLOW.

AUGUST

IF YOUR CAT IS SNORING, EXPECT FOUL WEATHER.

AUGUST HAS 31 DAYS.
The eighth month is named to honor the first Roman emperor (and grandnephew of Julius Caesar), Augustus Caesar (63 B.C.–A.D. 14).

THE FULL STURGEON MOON got its name from Native American tribes who found that sturgeon of the Great Lakes and Lake Champlain were most readily caught at this time.

BIRTHSTONE: PERIDOT
This gemstone symbolizes strength and was believed to protect wearers from nightmares.

POPPY

BIRTH FLOWERS: GLADIOLUS AND POPPY
Gladiolus says strength, while poppy means consolation (red) or success (yellow).

SKY HIGHS
An evening star is a planet that shines brightly in the western sky just after sunset. A morning star is one that shines brightly in the eastern sky just before sunrise.

AUGUST 4

COAST GUARD DAY
On this day in 1790, Secretary of the Treasury Alexander Hamilton ordered a fleet of 10 cutters (ships) to patrol the coast and reinforce tariff laws. In 1915, this organization became the Coast Guard, dedicated to saving lives at sea and enforcing U.S. laws.

AUGUST 10, 2010

The lowest temperature on Earth, −136°F, was recorded at the South Pole on this date.

THIRD MONDAY

YUKON (CANADA) DISCOVERY DAY
In 1896, George Washington Carmack discovered gold at Bonanza Creek near Dawson City, triggering a gold rush. Parades, games, food, and special events are held to celebrate.

AUGUST 13, 1878

Andrew Campbell, with his 13-year-old nephew, discovered the Luray Caverns in Virginia, when cold air rushing from a sinkhole extinguished his candle.

AUGUST 17, 2008

American swimmer Michael Phelps became the first person to win eight gold medals in a single Olympics.

SEPTEMBER

FROGS SINGING IN THE EVENING INDICATE FAIR WEATHER THE NEXT DAY.

SEPTEMBER HAS 30 DAYS.

September is from the Latin word *septem,* for "seven," because this was the seventh month of the early Roman calendar.

The **FULL CORN MOON** corresponds with the time of the corn harvest. The **HARVEST MOON,** occurring in September or October, is the full Moon nearest the autumnal equinox. At this time, the Moon rises only 30 minutes later each night, giving extra light after sunset for harvesting.

BIRTHSTONE: SAPPHIRE

Usually blue, this gemstone symbolizes trust.

BIRTH FLOWERS: ASTER AND MORNING GLORY

The aster signifies love, and the morning glory symbolizes affection.

ASTER

SKY HIGHS

The autumnal equinox occurs around September 22: Earth's two hemispheres receive the Sun's rays about equally; the Sun is overhead at noon as seen from the equator; and the amounts of nighttime and daytime (sunlight) are roughly equal to each other.

ALL MONTH

NATIONAL LIBRARY CARD MONTH
Do you have yours? Check with your friends to see if they have library cards. If any do not have one, go with them to the library and show them why they should get one and how to do so.

SEPTEMBER 9, 1954

At age 16, Canadian Marilyn Bell became the first person to swim across Lake Ontario. She covered 32 miles as the crow flies, but actually swam much farther because at times she was buffeted off-course by winds. Research how she trained to accomplish this feat.

SEPT. 18, 1830

In a 9-mile race near Baltimore, Maryland, America's first steam locomotive, *Tom Thumb*, had mechanical problems and lost to a horse.

SEPTEMBER 19, 2003

Frogs' eggs fell from the sky in Berlin, Connecticut.

SEPTEMBER 28, 1858

James Henry Fleming became the first in Canada to band a bird—a robin in his garden.

SEPTEMBER 24, 1905

Donati's Comet became the subject of the first comet photograph, taken by astronomers in Cambridge, Massachusetts. Named for Italian astronomer Giovanni Battista Donati, the comet had first been sighted from Florence, Italy, on June 2 of that year.

October

OCTOBER HAS 31 DAYS.

The 10th month takes it name from the Latin word *octo*, "eight," because this was the eighth month of the early Roman calendar.

The FULL HUNTER'S MOON occurs when the leaves are falling and the game animals have fattened. Now was the time for Native Americans to hunt and lay in a store of provisions for the long winter ahead.

SKY HIGHS

What's the farthest thing that you can see in the night sky with the naked eye? The Andromeda Galaxy—a galaxy far, far away, beyond our Milky Way.

BIRTHSTONE: OPAL

Opals can flash a rainbow of colors. The gem symbolizes hope and was once thought to improve eyesight.

BIRTH FLOWERS: COSMOS AND CALENDULA

Cosmos is a symbol of joy, and calendula represents grace.

COSMOS

CALENDULA

WHEN BIRDS AND BADGERS ARE FAT IN OCTOBER, EXPECT A COLD WINTER.

OCTOBER 5, 1984

As a member of NASA's *Challenger* shuttle crew, Marc Garneau became the first Canadian in space. He returned to orbit in 1996 and 2000, becoming the first Canadian to make three such journeys. Do research to learn more about Canada's astronauts.

SECOND TUESDAY

ADA LOVELACE DAY

Born in 1815, Ada at a young age was encouraged by her mother to study math. At 17, she explained how to create numerical codes that included repeating instructions—but her work was not discovered until the 1950s! Today, she is considered the first computer programmer, and the computer language "Ada" is named after her.

WEEK CONTAINING OCTOBER 10

NATIONAL METRIC WEEK

This is the week of October 10, the 10th day in the 10th month. In metric, the accepted standard of measurement around the world, 10 is a pivotal number. Work with a teacher to have a metric fair, with track events, cooking projects, scavenger hunts with metric maps, metric height and weight measurements, and more.

OCT. 29, 1969

At 10:30 P.M., a computer at UCLA sent a message to a computer at Stanford University, the first connection in a network that would lead to development of the Internet. Research to learn about the message.

NOVEMBER

NOVEMBER HAS 30 DAYS.
The name of our 11th month comes from the Latin word *novem,* "nine," because this was the ninth month of the early Roman calendar.

At this time of year, before the swamps froze, Native Americans set traps to catch beavers and ensure a supply of warm winter furs, so they called this full Moon the FULL BEAVER MOON.

A MONTH THAT COMES IN GOOD [WEATHERWISE] WILL GO OUT BAD.

BIRTHSTONE: TOPAZ
Topaz was once the name for any yellow gemstone. Ancient Greeks thought that it could make its wearer invisible.

BIRTH FLOWER: CHRYSANTHEMUM
Chrysanthemums represent cheerfulness.

SKY HIGHS
Around November 17 or 18, look up into the dark night sky for the Leonids meteor shower. Expect 10 to 15 shooting stars per hour!

NOVEMBER 6, 1861

James Naismith was born in Almonte, Ontario. When he was in his 30s, he invented the game of basketball, using peach baskets as nets. Do research to learn why he did this and how the game is different today.

NOVEMBER 19, 1493

DISCOVERY DAY, PUERTO RICO
Christopher Columbus "discovered" Puerto Rico. His crew named the island *San Juan Bautista* (for St. John the Baptist) and a town *Puerto Rico* (which means "rich port") because when they landed, the natives offered gold. Later, the names of the town and island were switched.

FRIDAY AFTER U.S. THANKSGIVING

NATIVE AMERICAN HERITAGE DAY
To recognize the rich culture, tradition, and history of Native Americans, read a book, watch a movie, or do research to learn more about Native Americans from your part of the country.

NOVEMBER 20, 1866

The yo-yo was patented on this day, but its invention dates from the ancient Greeks. Over the centuries, its popularity spread around the world. It is believed that its name comes from the Philippine word *yóyo*. A yo-yo was onboard NASA's space shuttle *Discovery* when it was launched on April 12, 1985.

LAST SUNDAY

MONKEY BUFFET FESTIVAL
In Lopburi, Thailand, wild monkeys are invited to a buffet of soda, sweets, fruit, nuts, and vegetables. It is a way to say thank you: Thai people believe that monkeys bring good fortune. Traditional music and dance are performed for human guests.

DECEMBER

IN WINTER, WHEN PIGS RUB UP AGAINST THEIR PENS, EXPECT A THAW.

BIRTHSTONE: TURQUOISE
This relatively "soft," greenish-blue stone was often worn for protection.

BIRTH FLOWERS: HOLLY AND NARCISSUS
Holly means happiness at home, while narcissus means that you love yourself.

NARCISSUS

DECEMBER HAS 31 DAYS.
The name of the 12th month comes from the Latin word *decem*, "ten," because this was originally the 10th month of the early Roman calendar.

At this time of year, the winter cold fastens its grip and the nights become long and dark, so Native Americans called this month's full Moon the FULL COLD MOON.

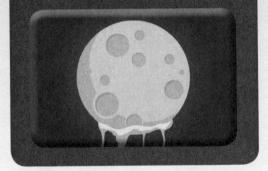

SKY HIGHS
The winter solstice (December 21 or 22) marks the first day of winter. The Sun rises and sets directly over the line known as the Tropic of Capricorn, and the Northern Hemisphere experiences its shortest period of daylight.

DECEMBER 7, 1898

The world's first Christmas postage stamp was released in Canada.

DECEMBER 14, 1807

At 6:30 A.M., people from Vermont to Connecticut saw a red fireball race across the sky, break apart, and fall to Earth—all in about 3 seconds. It was the first meteorite officially recorded in the New World.

DECEMBER 16, 1773

BOSTON TEA PARTY

On this night, a group of men calling themselves the Sons of Liberty boarded three ships in Boston Harbor and threw 342 chests of tea overboard in a rebellion against England's taxation of colonists without allowing them representation in government.

DECEMBER 19, 1871

Mark Twain received a patent for "Adjustable and Detachable Straps for Garments," a strap to make a snug fit of vest, shirts, and other clothes.

DECEMBER 26

BOXING DAY

This marks the Old English custom of giving to tradesmen, postmen, and servants Christmas "boxes" usually made of pottery and containing money. Today, where celebrated (such as in Canada), the holiday is usually marked by a gift of money placed in a greeting card and given beforehand. Make a thank-you card for your postman or other delivery service.

URANUS:
PLANET OF SURPRISES

THIS MUCH-TEASED, DRAB-LOOKING PLANET MAY SEEM LIKE NOTHING SPECIAL, BUT TAKE A CLOSER LOOK!

DISCOVERY

Uranus was the sixth planet to be discovered and the first one found with a telescope. English musician William Herschel, whose hobby was astronomy, detected the object on March 13, 1781. Others before him had thought that it was a star, but William noticed that it was moving very slowly and suggested that it might be a comet. Later research revealed that it was a planet. England's King George III, a science fan, was so pleased that he knighted William and appointed him court astronomer.

ASTRONOMY

HOW DO YOU SAY IT?

The cause of many blushes and giggles, Uranus's name is usually pronounced YUR-eh-nus, although yoo-RAY-nus is also used. William Herschel proposed calling it "Georgium Sidus" ("George's Star"), after King George III, but not many outside of England liked that idea. Ultimately, German astronomer Johann Bode suggested the winning name, which was based on mythology: Uranus is the Greek god of the sky. The name fit in nicely with those of the other five planets known at that time, which were all named after Roman gods.

VISIBILITY

Although very faint, Uranus can be seen with the naked eye, especially on clear, dark nights. You'll need sharp peepers: Its apparent magnitude is about 5.7.

LOCATION

Uranus is the seventh planet from the Sun, about 1.8 billion miles away.

AGE

About 4.5 billion years—the same as the Sun.

Convert to metric on p. 187

ORIENTATION

Uranus lies on its side as it rotates, at a nearly 98-degree tilt.

COLOR

Blue-green, due to methane in the upper atmosphere. The methane absorbs red light, leaving blue and green wavelengths to reach our eyes.

SIZE

Uranus is the third largest planet in the solar system. Its diameter of about 31,764 miles is four times that of Earth.

ROTATION

Uranus rotates clockwise, east to west. Venus is the only other planet to do so in our solar system.

YEAR

84 Earth years— that's how long it takes Uranus to complete one orbit around the Sun.

COOL FACT

Uranium, discovered in 1789, was named after the planet Uranus.

COMPOSITION

Uranus is an ice giant planet made up mostly of special ices. The planet's thick, layered atmosphere contains about 83 percent hydrogen, 15 percent helium, and 2 percent methane, with traces of water and ammonia. A high-altitude haze covers several layers of clouds. Scientists believe that the thick mantle below the atmosphere contains water, ammonia, and methane "ices" that are hot, dense, and fluid. In the center is likely a small, rocky core, which heats up to 9,000°F.

SEASONS

The planet has four seasons, each lasting 21 Earth years. For nearly a quarter of the planet's year, the Sun shines directly over one pole. It's currently spring in the northern hemisphere of Uranus, with summer arriving in 2028.

RINGS

13 known. The inner 11 rings are mostly dark and narrow. The two outer rings are reddish and blue.

HOLD YOUR NOSE!

Anyone approaching the upper atmosphere of Uranus would have plenty to deal with, not least of which would be toxic air and super-cold temperatures. Recently, scientists confirmed one more problem: smell. Thanks to the presence of hydrogen sulfide gas, the clouds in Uranus's upper atmosphere stink like rotten eggs.

DAY LENGTH

17 hours, 14 minutes—that's how long it takes for Uranus to rotate on its axis once.

WEATHER

Cold and windy. The average temperature is a numbing −357°F; the lowest recorded is −371°F. Winds are fierce, blowing up to 560 miles per hour. Research suggests that it rains diamonds in the mantle layer.

VISITORS

Only one so far. After a 9-year journey, on January 24, 1986, NASA's *Voyager 2* spacecraft swept by, gathering data.

MOONS

27, but it's likely that more will be found. The outer five moons (Ariel, Miranda, Oberon, Titania, Umbriel) are the largest, with Titania topping out at 981 miles in diameter. (Earth's Moon is 2,159 miles wide.) All of the moons of Uranus have names from plays by William Shakespeare or verse by Alexander Pope.

JOURNEY
THROUGH THE
CENTER
OF EARTH

It takes between 12 and 36 hours to fly from North America to China, depending on the number of stops and the length of the layovers. But what if you could get there another way? Here are some *simple* instructions for digging a tunnel to China.

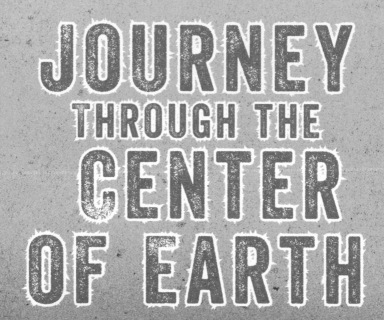

FIND A DIGGING TOOL.

You'll need something better than a shovel to do your digging. It will have to be able to pierce Earth's rocky crust, which is anywhere from 3 to 43 miles thick. The deepest hole ever dug, the Kola Superdeep Borehole in Russia, went down only 7½ miles. It was dug using a giant drill.

2

Convert to metric on p. 187

1

START IN THE RIGHT PLACE.

For every place on Earth, there is a spot on the opposite side of the planet that is called its "antipode." If you could dig a tunnel straight through the center of Earth, that's the spot where you would come out. For example, if you started your tunnel almost anywhere in North America, you would come out in the Indian Ocean. (Make sure to bring a snorkel.) If you want to go to Wuhu, China, you'll have to start at its antipode in Rafaela, Argentina—so, first make sure that you can speak some Spanish.

3

TINKER WITH THE LAWS OF PHYSICS.

There are still a few problems to work out before starting your trip. Things like stopping Earth from rotating while you're in the tunnel, figuring out a way to breathe in there, and inventing some kind of pressure suit to wear so that you don't come out looking like a flatworm. Let's put those aside for now. You'll think of something.

4

LOOK OUT, BELOW!

Dive into your hole. You'll start falling at 32 feet per second per second, eventually reaching a speed of 18,000 miles per hour halfway through the ride (which will take about 42 minutes in all).

5

GET READY TO TAKE SOME HEAT.

You'll want to wear your asbestos outerwear (and underwear), because the temperature in your tunnel will go up about 15 degrees Fahrenheit for every mile that you dig down. The scientists digging the Kola hole had to stop because the temperature at the bottom of the hole reached 356°F and the drill stopped working. If you figure out how to drill deeper, you'll still have to go through the upper mantle. This is a gooey layer with an average thickness of 1,800 miles, at temperatures ranging from 932°F at the top to 7,200°F at the bottom, where it meets Earth's outer core—which itself is 1,400 miles of molten iron and nickel as hot as the surface of the Sun (11,000°F). Then you'll get to drill through Earth's inner core, a solid metal ball about 70 percent the size of the Moon. Good luck.

Convert to metric on p. 187

7 PREPARE FOR LANDING.

Once you get past the center of Earth, you'll be traveling uphill, against the force of gravity, and this will slow you down. In fact, when you reach the surface in China, you'll come to a stop and start falling back down! So, be sure to have someone there to catch you! Pick someone who can speak Chinese.

6 DO IT ALL OVER AGAIN BUT IN REVERSE.

Now that you're at the center of Earth, all you have to do is get up to the surface in China. But remember, not only will you have to make this hole long enough to reach the other side of Earth (nearly 8,000 miles), but also you'll have to figure out what to do with all of the stuff that you dug out and where to put it back in Argentina. No vacuum cleaner will help with this mess! But it's not all bad news: You'll feel cooler the closer you get to the surface.

Sound impossible? You're probably right. But let's face it: Your biggest problem is likely how to get to Argentina in the first place!

OUT-OF-THIS-WORLD GARDENING

Many of the same vegetables that you grow in your garden on Earth are being grown in outer space.

Any planet is a long way from Earth, and providing enough food for astronauts who will be spending years on another planet will be difficult. One idea is to grow fruit and vegetables in outer space, so astronauts are perfecting the technique on the International Space Station (ISS).

Grade 6 students in London, Ontario, plant Tomatosphere seeds with Canadian astronaut Jeremy Hansen.

Plants being tested for possible growth on the ISS.

SPACE GARDEN NEEDS

Plants need to be grown differently in spacecraft due to the absence of gravity, sunlight, and wind. To keep the soil from floating away, seeds are planted in small packets of claylike soil. The lack of sunshine requires using fluorescent or LED lights, just as many gardeners do on Earth when starting seeds in the dark days of winter. Fans act as wind by gently circulating air around the plants to prevent mold and strengthen their stems. Space gardens can't be watered with a watering can or hose, so plastic tubes carry water directly to the plant roots.

The plants and astronauts have a symbiotic relationship, meaning that they help each other. When humans exhale carbon dioxide, plants absorb it. The plants, in turn, give off oxygen, which humans need. Some human waste (urine and feces) is treated and used to feed and water the plants. The plants then give off clean water vapor through transpiration, which the astronauts can collect and drink.

STARTING WITH SEEDS

Scientists first began experimenting with space gardening in 1971, when they sent tree seeds around the Moon and back to expose them to the heat and energy outside Earth's atmosphere. Upon their return, the seeds were inspected and planted, and no changes were found.

Twelve years later, 40 different varieties of fruit and vegetable seeds went into space. When they arrived back on Earth, the seeds were planted. Some seeds appeared slightly different, but the vegetables that grew were safe to eat. A few of the plants grew faster and larger than usual, but most grew into ordinary plants.

After trying for several years, astronauts finally succeeded in growing small zucchini, sunflower, and broccoli plants in plastic bags in 2012 on the ISS. In 2014, they grew and harvested lettuce, which was then frozen and returned to Earth to be tested for safety. Now they grow mostly lettuce aboard the ISS and eat the fresh greens. Watching plants grow reminds the astronauts of home, which improves their moods and helps with homesickness.

Right, the 'Veggie' plant station being tested at Kennedy Space Center in Florida; below, NASA astronaut Steve Swanson harvests a crop of lettuce grown on the space station.

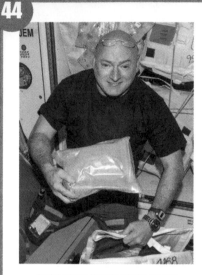

Astronaut Scott Kelly holds 600,000 tomato seeds for distribution to classes in the U.S. and Canada.

FROM SPACE TO SCHOOLS

You can grow space seeds on Earth—maybe. A project called Tomatosphere gives students the opportunity to grow tomato seeds that may have been to space. Seeds that visited the ISS are distributed to participating classrooms along with seeds that did not travel into space. Students plant the seeds and monitor their growth, but they don't learn which seeds went into space until their project ends. In 2017, over 24,000 classrooms signed up to participate! Ask your teacher if your class can be part of the next Tomatosphere project. For more information, go to www .firsttheseedfoundation.org/tomatosphere.

FAR OUT!

- In 2006, Russia presented China with seeds that had been on the space station *Mir* for 6 years. According to Chinese sources, a few of the seeds grew larger-than-normal vegetables. These plants were then bred with others that also grew larger vegetables. After 4 years of breeding these super plants together, the resulting plants regularly grew jumbo vegetables, such as 21-pound tomatoes, 2-foot-long cucumbers, and pumpkins 10 times the normal size. Breeders say that a lot of these huge vegetables have more vitamins and better

flavor than their Earthbound relatives.
- In 2008, a cherry tree seed from Japan that had orbited Earth produced a tree that grew faster than usual and bloomed 6 years early. Its blossoms have five petals instead of what should be 30!

SPACE-AGE TAKE-OUT

Early astronauts ate baby food packed in toothpaste-like tubes by squeezing the food into their mouths. Now on the ISS, the food is much like ours—they even eat pizza! Fresh fruit and vegetables can be eaten without preparation, but other food arrives fully cooked, packaged in small pouches, and requiring only heating. Astronauts tear the top off a food pouch and eat slowly with a spoon. If they lift the spoon too fast, when it stops, the food will float off and have to be captured. They drink from a pouch through a straw with a shutoff lever, which prevents the liquid from floating out between sips. Supplies and food arrive by unmanned space vessels. Food is provided to the astronauts by their own countries, but any special treats—such as candy—are shared among the crew.

Astronaut Peggy Whitson enjoys a hamburger in the
Service Module of the ISS.

Weather Mysteries
SOLVED!

WEATHER

The Case of the Killer Fog

On December 5, 1952, fog rolled over the city of London. Fog is common in London, but there was something strange about this one. A few hours after the fog arrived, it turned a dark, murky color as it mixed with soot from smokestacks and chimneys. Soon, being outside became unsafe. The air smelled of rotten eggs. People could not see through the fog and held on to buildings for help while walking. Roads and sidewalks were covered with what looked like grease. When people came inside, they found their faces covered and nostrils filled with a black film. The toxic fog killed thousands of people and didn't lift for 5 days.

Why was this fog different? A high-pressure weather system had stalled over London. This caused a temperature inversion, meaning that a layer of warm air high above the surface had trapped the cold December air at ground level. This prevented the sulfurous coal smoke from smokestacks and chimneys from rising, and there was no wind to move the soot-filled fog. A substance called sulfuric acid formed in the fog and poisoned the city.

THE CASE OF THE SMOKY AIR

On Sunday, September 21, 2014, at about 6:30 A.M., 1,755 people assembled on Kings Beach on the northern shore of Lake Tahoe in California. In about 2 minutes, they would begin the Ironman Triathlon, swimming 2.4 miles, biking 112 miles, and then running a marathon (26.2 miles) over mountainous terrain. When the announcer began to speak, they expected him to say "Go!," but instead he said "Canceled."

What happened? For days, the air had been full of smoke from the devastating King Fire, which had started on September 13 and eventually burned more than 97,000 drought-stricken acres over the next 27 days. Event officials had decided that the smoke was hazardous to human health. The poor air quality had also forced the cancellation of school soccer games and recess and children's outdoor activities.

Convert to metric on p. 187

SOLVED!

The Case of the Orange Snow

On the morning of March 24, 2018, the mountains of Sochi, Russia, and parts of Bulgaria, Ukraine, and Romania were covered with orange snow. The orange layer was not deep: Skiers and snowboarders traversing the slopes pushed the orange snow aside to reveal white snow underneath.

What caused this? The jet stream had brought a series of storms to the Sahara Desert in northern Africa. The winds picked up the desert's orange sand and dust and blew it into the cold upper atmosphere, where it mixed with snow and rain. As the jet stream pushed the storms north over eastern Europe, the weight of the icy sand and dust particles caused them to fall as snow.

SOLVED!

THE CASE OF THE BENT TREES

The southernmost part of New Zealand's South Island, Slope Point, is pastureland that ends at the Southern Ocean and is only 2,982 miles from the South Pole. There are no houses on the rolling landscape, and the only natural growth other than grass is a small forest of tangled cypress trees that grow sideways.

Why sideways? The trees were planted in the 1800s to shelter a home from the fierce, cold Antarctic winds that whip across the land. The pressure of the wind all day, every day, pushed the trees into their crooked position. The house disappeared years ago, and today the trees provide shelter for sheep that graze there.

SOLVED!

The Case of the Pink Snow

In 1818, a fleet of ships from England was on its way to the Arctic Circle. Captain John Ross was given the task of finding a passage to the Pacific Ocean and charting the northern coast of North America. Harsh weather caused the ships to abandon their expedition and head home. As they sailed past Greenland, Captain Ross spied pinkish red–streaked snow. He ordered crew members to gather samples of the oddity. Analysis of the snow in England suggested that iron deposits had caused the pink tinge—but this conclusion was found to be incorrect.

What was it? Many years later, the real cause of the colored snow was discovered. Snow algae called Chlamydomonas nivalis, *which thrive in cold conditions, had caused a chemical reaction with the snow. Although the algae look green under a microscope, when they are exposed to sunlight, they turn pinkish red. The result of this interaction is often called "watermelon snow" because of its color and sweet smell.*

THE CASE OF
THE CROOKED FOREST

Near Gryfino, Poland, about 400 pine trees bend near the ground, so that their trunks grow sideways for 4 to 9 feet before straightening out to grow upward as high as 50 feet. All of the bent trunks in the Crooked Forest point northward.

How could this happen? There is no straight answer for why or how the trees developed their shape. One idea is that a heavy snow weighed down the trees when they were saplings. However, most observers believe that farmers put weight on the trees to make them bend so that their wood could be used for furniture, for building ships, or for use by oxen as yokes for pulling plows.

Convert to metric on p. 187

SOLVED?

Adrift on

A tale of courage,

On Easter Sunday, April 19, 1908, the town of St. Anthony, Newfoundland, Canada, was locked in the grip of winter even though it was spring. Ice and snow lay thick and heavy. As Dr. Wilfred Grenfell walked to the hospital, he got word that he was needed in a village about 60 miles to the south.

The doctor gathered instruments, dressings, and medicine, as well as food and clothing, and harnessed his seven best dogs—Moody, Watch, Spy, Doc, Brin, Jerry, and Sue—to his komatik. With his pet spaniel, Jack, for company, Dr. Grenfell set out for Lock's Cove, the first leg of the journey, 20 miles south on Hare Bay.

That night, as the doctor rested at Lock's Cove, fog rolled in and rain fell, softening the snow. A northeast wind and stormy sea pushed huge

NEWFOUND TERMS

Bight: a bend in a coast, forming an open bay
Ice pan: a floating piece of ice
Komatik: a sled with wooden runners, lashed together with rawhide
Landwash: the area between the high- and low-tide marks
Oilskins: a heavy cotton raincoat or outerwear treated with oil as waterproofing
Shoal: a sandbank or sandbar that creates shallow water
Sish: tiny bits of ice, often the result of large pans pounding together
Slob: sludgy masses of floating ice
Traces: harness lines

the Ice
skill, and survival

chunks of ice onto the landwash and created ice pans in the open water.

In the morning, Dr. Grenfell noticed that conditions had created a shortcut. A natural ice bridge connected the cove to an island 3 miles offshore. From there, it was 4 miles across the ice to the southern shore. To save time, Dr. Grenfell decided to take this route.

The team made it to the island safely and began the final stretch. When they were about a quarter-mile from the shore, the wind died and the ice beneath the komatik became sish. Moments later, the wind began to blow from offshore, the sish became slob, and the ice field broke into a pond of ice pans, each about 10 feet square.

Dr. Grenfell pulled off his heavy gear—oilskins, hat, coat, and gloves—and shouted to his team to run for the shore. The harder the dogs pulled, the

WITH A HEAVY HEART, HE QUICKLY
SACRIFICED THREE OF THE DOGS.

deeper their paws and the komatik sank into the soft slob. After going only about 20 feet, the team stopped. The slob was giving way under their weight.

Concerned that the dogs would become tangled in their traces, Dr. Grenfell jumped into the frigid water and cut their lines. He climbed onto an ice pan, dragged the dogs up on it with him, and almost immediately realized that it would not hold them all.

A larger, more solid pan floated about 20 yards away. The sled dogs, weighted with water, refused to follow Dr. Grenfell's command to swim to it. What to do? Make a game of it! As if playing fetch, Dr. Grenfell tossed a small piece of ice like a stick and Jack went into the water after it, with the sled dogs not far behind.

By now, Dr. Grenfell's remaining clothing—flannel shirt, sweater-vest, soccer shorts, socks, and boots—was soaking wet. After cutting off his boots, he fashioned a jacket for protection and then took off his clothes and swung them in the air to dry. This was not enough.

TO THE RESCUE

That Monday evening, four men had been on Ireland's Point, above the Bight, and seen something unusual on the water. They notified the only man in the village who owned a telescope, and he confirmed the sight of a man adrift on a pan. Being dusk, it was too late to launch a rescue, so the five men put out first thing in the morning. Dr. Grenfell was taken to St. Anthony, where he was treated for frostbite on his hands and feet. The patient whom he was on his way to see was also brought to St. Anthony and survived. Soon after being rescued, Dr. Grenfell hung a bronze plaque on a wall in his home that read:

TO THE MEMORY OF
Three Noble Dogs
MOODY
WATCH
SPY
Whose Lives Were Given for Mine on the Ice
April 21st, 1908

With a heavy heart, he quickly sacrificed three of the dogs. He clothed himself in their skins, piled their bodies to block the wind, and curled up with the remaining dogs.

He slept, but woke up shivering in the dark. His clothing was stiff, his fingers were frozen, and his wet feet were extremely cold. He needed help! He tied together two of his dead dogs' leg bones as a staff and attached his shirt as a flag. He planned to wave it after sunrise.

By morning, the ice raft had drifted near Ireland's Bight, a fishing station that Dr. Grenfell knew was deserted at this time of year. He did not expect help to come from there, and he was getting hungry. He began to think about eating one of the dogs for food. Suddenly, in the distance, Dr. Grenfell saw a boat!

Within minutes, the boat drew nearer. The rescuers on board called out and waved. Soon, the doctor and the dogs were safe aboard. Through it all, Dr. Grenfell later said, he had never felt afraid.

Let It Snow!

Do you love snow days?
Or are you a snowbird?
A snowbird is someone
who heads south (usually
to Florida) every winter to
avoid cold and snow. (But the
snowbirds of 1977 got a big
surprise when flakes fell as far
south as Miami Beach!)

Q:
What do you get when
you cross a snowman
with a vampire?
A:
Frostbite

In 1921, Silver Lake, Colorado, set the record for the most snow to fall in a 24-hour period: 75.8 inches!

What Is That Stuff?

Clouds are made up of tiny water droplets. When these droplets start to freeze, ice crystals form. As the crystals fall, they often collect more droplets that freeze and stick together. A snowflake can be made up of just one ice crystal or many. Most snowflakes are less than ½ inch across.

Sometimes, with just the right conditions—like little or no wind, which tears them apart—snowflakes can get big. William S. Pike of Great Britain's Royal Meteorological Society says that temperatures just above freezing (32°F or 0°C) help snowflakes to grow.

Measuring snowflakes is tricky but not impossible. Here's how to do it:

- Try to find a spot away from the wind.
- Collect falling snowflakes on a black piece of construction paper.
- Use a magnifying glass to observe them closely.
- Using a ruler, measure quickly. Be careful not to breathe on the snowflakes.
- Snap a picture of large snowflakes beside the ruler to show their size.

According to Guinness World Records, the largest snowflakes fell in January 1887, during a storm at Fort Keogh, Montana. One rancher called the snowflakes "larger than milk pans" and measured a flake at 15 inches wide.

Convert to metric on p. 187

Fake Flake

Christa Faye Hanson made the world's largest paper snowflake in Kanawha, Iowa, on September 3, 2012. The flake measured 14 feet 6 inches across.

World Record!
World's Largest Paper Snowflake
Created by Christa Hanson September 3, 2012 Kanawha, Iowa
← Over 14 Feet Across →

FRIGHTFUL STUFF

Fear of snow is called **chionophobia.**

Fear of cold is called **cryophobia.**

Fear of freezing rain is called **pluvifrigophobia.**

Make Snow Ice Cream

You will need:
8 cups of fresh, white snow
5 tablespoons sugar
1 teaspoon vanilla extract*
dash of cinnamon
milk

Put the snow into a cold bowl. Add sugar, vanilla, and cinnamon. Stir, adding milk a little at a time until the frozen treat reaches a consistency to your liking. Then scoop it up!
Experiment by using a different flavor of extract, such as lemon, coconut, or mint.

THE UNFORGETTABLES

The Great Blizzard of 1888, a surprise storm on March 11 and 12, dumped 40 to 55 inches of snow from Washington, D.C., to Maine. Houses were buried, trains were stopped, and 200 ships sank.

Tamarack, California, a tiny place in the Sierra Mountains, holds the record for the most snow in a calendar month. In January 1911, it was buried by 390 inches of snow. That's 32½ feet!

Parts of eastern Canada plus 26 states in the U.S. experienced the 1993 **"Storm of the Century."** The March storm left 50 or more inches of snow in some areas.

A blizzard hit the mid-Atlantic and northeastern states so hard in January 2016 that people began calling the storm **"Snowzilla."** One of the highest amounts of snow was recorded in Glengary, West Virginia—42 inches!

Eyes on the Snow

Scientists study the amount of snow on the ground to measure how changes affect climate, glaciers, and water supplies. Snow cover influences Earth's temperature, and melting snow helps to fill bodies of water. World snowfall amounts are important to people using water for things like farming and making electricity.

A satellite mission called Global Precipitation Measurement (GPM) evaluates rain and snowfall around the world every 3 hours. NASA and Japan's space agency launched the satellite on February 27, 2014. GPM data help scientists to better understand Earth's water and energy cycles and improve weather forecasting.

Q: What is a snowman's favorite lunch?

A: Icebergers

SNOWMAN SPECIALISTS

Building the perfect snowman is harder than it looks. Just ask the engineering students at Bluefield State College in West Virginia, who have studied this very subject. Their professor, Roy Pruett, says that 30°F is the perfect temperature for snowman-building. Colder temperatures can make snow too dry to pack together. Warmer temperatures make for mushy snow that doesn't hold its shape.

Marc Asperas likes to build large snowmen, and he has a secret to his success. He starts by constructing hollow spheres and rolls them in snow. At first, he had a problem—the snow slid right off! Then Marc came up with a magic solution: He covered the spheres with Legos! The snow packed perfectly between the pieces and held tight. This technique helped him to build a 7-foot-high snowman on top of Zugspitze, Germany's tallest mountain. He now holds a patent for an "Apparatus for Facilitating the Construction of a Snow Man/Woman."

SNOW REPORT

A **snow crystal** is a single crystal of ice.

A snowflake can be either a single ice crystal or a clump of crystals that falls from the sky.

Sleet forms when raindrops freeze into small, semi-clear ice balls before reaching the ground.

Freezing rain occurs when supercooled rain hits a surface with a temperature below freezing. It coats things such as trees, cars, and roads with a layer of ice.

Graupel forms when supercooled water droplets freeze on snowflakes. These snow pellets are cloudy, not clear.

Hail forms when droplets of water freeze together in the cold clouds of a thunderstorm.

A **flurry** is snow that falls for only a short time, with little or no accumulation.

A **snow bomb cyclone** results from "bombogenesis," the quick intensification of a snowstorm caused by the air pressure at its center dropping at least 24 millibars in 24 hours. These storms are capable of producing hurricane-force winds.

Thunder snow is snow that occurs with thunder and lightning.

Snow showers fall at different rates for a short time, sometimes with accumulation.

A **snow squall** is a brief, intense, heavy snowfall with strong winds and often accumulation.

A **blizzard** is a fierce storm that occurs when a large amount of snow is accompanied by strong winds (35 mph or more) and low visibility (less than ¼ mile) for at least 3 hours.

It All Started With Halloween

Scientists have been naming hurricanes and tropical storms in the United States since 1953. The World Meteorological Organization chooses the names.

In 2011, forecasters at The Weather Channel (TWC) nicknamed a Halloween storm "Snowtober." The next winter, TWC came up with an alphabetized list of names for winter storms, beginning with Athena and ending with Zeus.

A high school Latin teacher in Bozeman, Montana, showed her class the list. One student joked that they should come up with their own list, and they did! They created 4 years' worth of Greek and Roman names for winter storms and sent them to the channel. TWC used many of their names and continued to consult with the school's Latin classes for several years. As a thank-you, TWC named a storm "Bozeman."

Snow Day?

When David Sukhin was a middle-school student in New Jersey, he obsessed over school being canceled due to snow. In high school, he invented a "Snow Day Calculator" (now an app) to make predictions. David developed a formula that takes into account things like the amount of snow expected, storm timing, and a school district's history of cancellations. Students type in their zip code and a few more things, such as whether their school is public or private. David's calculator has been wildly popular and highly accurate.

- When the first snowflakes are large, the snowstorm will be a lasting one. When they are small, the storm will be a short one.
- *The north wind doth blow, And we shall have snow.*
- *If snow begins at mid of day, Expect a foot of it to lay.*

ONLY IN ANTARCTICA

You've heard of sand dunes, but what about snow dunes? Centuries of nonstop wind in Antarctica have formed snow megadunes that sometimes can reach as high as 26 feet. These immense waves of snow cover an area about the size of California. They form unusual rippling patterns. From space, they look like giant fingerprints.

ARE YOU ON CLOUD NINE OR IN A FOG?

Many expressions, or idioms, are connected to the weather.
For example, "When it rains, it pours" means that misfortunes tend
to occur at the same time. See if you can match the following
weather expressions with their meanings.

1. To get wind of something.

2. Every cloud has a silver lining.

3. To be in a fog.

4. As right as rain.

5. To break the ice.

6. To steal someone's thunder.

7. To have your head in the clouds.

8. To rain on their parade.

9. To be on thin ice.

10. To be a ray of sunshine.

11. To be on cloud nine.

12. To weather the storm.

13. To be under the weather.

A. To be extremely happy.

B. To be confused or dazed.

C. To find out about something.

D. The idea that good can come from even a bad situation.

E. To be in a risky or dangerous position.

F. To get through a difficult time.

G. To be impractical, unrealistic, fanciful.

H. To ruin someone else's good mood or plans.

I. To say or do something to ease a stressful or awkward situation.

J. To bring happiness to someone else.

K. To feel like yourself again after being ill.

L. To say or do something before someone was about to say or do the same thing.

M. To not feel well.

Answers: 1. C; 2. D; 3. B; 4. K; 5. I; 6. L; 7. G; 8. H; 9. E; 10. J; 11. A; 12. F; 13. M

SCRAMBLED FACTS ABOUT CHICKENS

WHO'S WHO IN THE COOP

Hen: a female chicken
Rooster: a male chicken
Chick: a baby chicken
Pullet: a female chicken less than 1 year old
Cockerel: a male chicken less than 1 year old
Brood: baby chickens, or to care for chicks
Broody hen: a hen that covers her eggs to warm and hatch them
Flock: a group of birds, such as chickens, that live together
Fowl: a bird of any kind, but often more specifically a domesticated bird kept for its eggs and flesh

THIS WILL CRACK YOU UP

- It's hard to outrun a chicken. They can run as fast as 9 miles per hour, while humans average just over 8 miles per hour.

- *Most breeds of chickens have four toes, but some have five.*

- Chickens can not see in the dark.

- *Chickens do not sweat. They regulate body temperature through their combs and wattles.*

- Chickens use their barbed tongues to catch food and move it to the back of the throat.

- *Chickens produce saliva, but they have few taste buds and can not taste sweetness.*

- The average chicken has 7,500 to 9,000 feathers. These are made of keratin, the same protein that is in human hair and fingernails.

- *The heart of a chicken beats about 400 times per minute; a human heart beats an average of 60 to 80 times per minute.*

- A chicken's earlobe indicates the color of its eggs: Red earlobes usually mean brown eggs; white earlobes usually mean white eggs.

- *The chicken is the closest living relative to Tyrannosaurus rex.*

INCREDIBLE EGGS

A hen can lay one egg approximately once every 26 hours. The average hen lays 265 eggs per year. This ability starts when the hen is around 18 to 20 weeks old and may continue for her entire life—as long as she is fertile and has proper nutrition and 14 hours of real or simulated daylight. Hens usually lay fewer eggs as they get older, beginning when they are about 2 years old.

HA! HA!

How did the hen graduate from college?
With egg-cellent grades.

CLICKING CHICKENS

Mother hens and their chicks talk to each other when the chicks are still in their shells. The chicks usually "speak" first. Twenty-four hours before they hatch, they make a "peep" or clicking sound. (Chicks in nearby eggs hear it, too.) The peeps tell the hen how long to stay on the nest and how many chicks to expect.

CHICKEN CHAT

Chickens use language to communicate about food, warn of predators or other threats, and talk among themselves. This language is used by all chickens, starting at about 14 weeks of age.

***Buh-dup,* or "Hi, there!"**
Hens greet other members of the flock with this, as they come and go during the day. They also say it to humans.

***SCREEE-oop-oop-oop,* or "Help!"**
When a broody hen feels threatened on her nest, she yells this, a noise that ends in a grumble.

***Bwah, bwah, bwah, bwah,* or "Egg on the way!"**
This is how a hen announces that she is ready to lay an egg.

***Buh-gaw-gawk, Buh-gaw-gawk, Buh-gaw-gawk,* or "I laid an egg!"**
After laying an egg, a hen celebrates her accomplishment by saying this loudly!

***Doh-doh-doh,* or "I'm here, and I'm okay."**
This is a hen's way of saying "Good night."

***Ur, ur, ur, UR-URRR,* or "Pay attention!"**
A rooster may crow at any hour of the day or night (not just in the morning) to let everybody know that he's there and to warn of possible threats.

FOLKLORE'S FEATHER WEATHER

Expect rain if a chicken . . .
• takes dust baths and seems uneasy
• spreads and ruffles its tail feathers
• goes to bed earlier than usual

Expect cold if a chicken . . .
• stands on one leg
• sits on the ground with all of its feathers ruffled

WHY THE CHICKEN DID NOT FLY ACROSS THE ROAD

Chickens are not great fliers. At best, they can get about 6 feet into the air and fly for a distance of about 20 feet. This is because chickens' ancestors lived on the ground and found food on the jungle floor; they did not search for it from the air like other birds did. Their relatively long legs and feet enabled them to walk and scratch, but their wings were strong enough only to carry them into nearby trees to roost. Flying capabilities have been bred out of today's domesticated chickens in favor of boosting their egg or meat production.

FOWL PLAY

Chickens clean themselves by playing in dirt. They take what's called a dust bath. A chicken will dig a hole large enough to sit in—or even a bit bigger so that another hen can join in. Each

hen rolls, scratches, stretches, and tosses the dirt into the air so that it falls onto their bodies. Eventually, gritty particles get under their feathers. This helps to control pests and parasites such as mites and poultry lice.

After cleaning itself with dust, a chicken reaches her beak back to her oil-filled uropygial (yoo-ruh-PIE-jee-ul) gland near her tail. She collects a bit of the oil and coats her feathers with it. This helps to repel water, keep the feathers clean, and prolong the life of each feather.

BITS ABOUT THE BEAK

A chicken's beak acts like a human's hand. It has a lot of sensory nerves and touch receptors. It is used for gathering food (including catching prey), courting, raising young, fighting, preening, and moving objects.

Chickens rub their beaks on hard objects such as logs and stones in order to clean, sharpen, and shape them. A chicken's beak grows throughout all of its life, so it needs to be trimmed—just like your fingernails.

HA! HA!

How do chickens
bake a cake?

From scratch.

WHICH CAME FIRST?

A question posed and debated for centuries is "Which came first, the chicken or the egg?"

Modern scientists now agree that thousands of years ago, two chicken-like birds got together and produced an egg from which hatched a bird that resembles today's chicken. Because the protein that builds the eggshell is made by the hen, scientists have determined that the chicken had to come before the egg. Without the hen, there would be no egg.

HAIL TO THE CHICKEN-IN-CHIEF!

Dominant hens, especially the head hen, are usually the teachers within the flock. They are the ones who try new foods and share them with the flock. They explore more and figure things out. For example, a dominant hen would be the first in the flock to learn how to open a critter-free feeder: It would figure out that it had to step on a plate to get to the feed. When a dominant hen discovers something new, the other hens observe and copy her behavior.

HA! HA!

How do baby chicks dance?
Chick to chick.

SECRETS OF A BLUE-RIBBON POULTRY PRIZEWINNER

In 2003, a chicken raised by 12-year-old Catherine Seltzer received first prize in a 4-H county fair competition. Here's Catherine's advice to other kid contestants on chicken "beauty tips":

• Wash the chicken with a mild detergent, then rinse with lemon juice and water. This will bring out the highlights in the feathers.

• Rub a combination of canola oil and rosemary on the hen's legs and feet to make them shine.

Convert to metric on p. 187

Eggs to Dye For

You can dye eggs naturally with spices, fruit, and vegetables!

Here are some dyes to try (but you should experiment, too):

FOR EACH EGG COLOR, YOU'LL NEED:
2 cups water
dye ingredient
1 tablespoon white vinegar
white hard-boiled eggs
pot
colander
bowl
spoon
paper towels

POSSIBLE DYE INGREDIENTS:
2 cups onion skins for orange
1 tablespoon ground turmeric for yellow
1 cup chopped purple or red cabbage
 for purple
1 cup blueberries for blue
2 cups spinach for green
1 cup shredded beets for pink

1. In a small pot, bring water and one dye ingredient to a boil, then turn the heat down to medium-low for 30 minutes.

2. Strain water into a bowl and stir in vinegar. Put eggs into the water. The longer they sit, the more vivid the color.

3. When desired color has been achieved, remove eggs and let dry on paper towels.

DELIGHTFUL

Q:
What do you call a goat dressed as a clown?
A:
A silly billy

You've Goat to Know . . .
A male goat is called a buck or billy.
A female goat is called a doe or nanny.
A baby goat is called a kid.
A group of goats is called a herd.

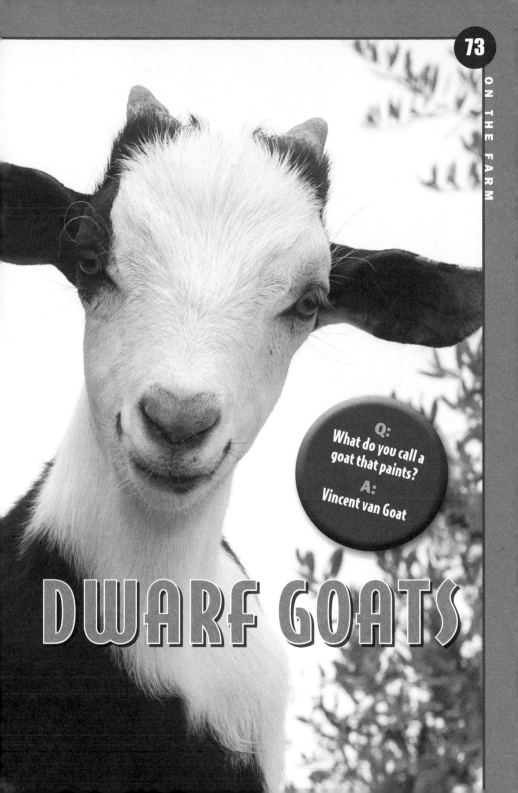

Q:
What do you call a
goat that paints?
A:
Vincent van Goat

DWARF GOATS

People have raised and used goats for over 8,000 years. Today, at least 210 different breeds make up the more than 400 million goats worldwide. Perhaps none is as charming as the friendly and affectionate Nigerian dwarf goat. This breed of goats showed up in the United States about 60 years ago, imported from West Africa. They love to be with people and other animals and are calm, playful, and easy to train.

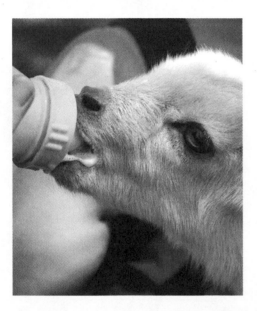

Kid Stuff

Nigerian dwarf goats weigh only about 2 pounds when born, and a doe will give birth to a litter of one to four kids. The kids are strong and can start running when they are only 1 to 2 minutes old!

When all grown up, they are 16 to 24 inches tall at the withers (shoulders), making them about half the size of a typical goat. They can live for up to 15 years.

Fancy Fur

These pretty goats have soft fur that can be black, chocolate brown, gold, or a combination of colors. They may have markings on their fur like freckles or stripes. Sometimes bucks grow long hair, including really long beards. Does may grow beards, too.

Eyes Spy

Goats are able to rotate their eyes in almost any direction, which comes in handy when they bow their heads to eat. Their rectangular pupils and eye movement abilities allow them to see animals coming from anywhere. This keeps them safe from becoming an enemy's prey. They like to eat hay and plants, including pesky poison ivy and prickly plants with thorns on them.

Match Up

Connect each goat-related phrase with its meaning:

1. to get your goat
2. to act the goat
3. G.O.A.T.
4. a scapegoat

a. Greatest of All Time
b. to annoy you or make you angry
c. a person who gets blamed for mistakes
d. to behave in a silly way

Answers: 1. b.; 2. d.; 3. a.; 4. c.

Knock. Knock.
Who's there?
Goat.
Goat who?
Goat to the door
and find out!

Got Goat Milk?

Nigerian dwarf does can be milked, and they produce a lot of it—up to 2 quarts, or 2½ pounds, per day! Their milk is creamy and sweet and has three times more butterfat than milk from other dairy goats. Worldwide, more people drink goat milk than any other variety. It is nutritious and easier to digest than cow's milk.

People also use the milk to make soaps and lotions. The extra butterfat provides more moisture for these products, making them very healthy for human skin.

No Kidding

Does and calm bucks are often trained as therapy animals, due to their gentle nature. They help people of all ages in hospitals, nursing homes, schools, and other places. They aid those who are in pain, need to calm down, are unhappy or worried, or just need a friend.

Matilda, aka "YZ"

Kids Helping Kids

Myranda Burress and her brother Joey live with their parents on a small farm in Oklahoma. They raise many animals, including Nigerian dwarf goats. Myranda and Joey help their dad build shelters for the goats, clean up after them, and feed them. (Their goats' favorite snack is corn chips!) These mild-mannered animals do not like to be alone, so Myranda and Joey make sure that all of the goats have companions.

One of their does, Mayflower, gave birth to three kids—two males and a female. Myranda and Joey are keeping the female kid as a pet. They named her Matilda but call her "YZ" because of her markings. On one side of YZ, you can see a white fur "Y." On her other side, there is a white fur "Z".

A Farmer's Life for Me!

**Twelve-year old Quinten Albrecht lives
with his mother, father, and sister
on a farm in rural Alberta, Canada. Here
he offers us a glimpse of his life.**

Farming runs in my blood like oil runs in an engine. I come from a long line of farmers and feel very lucky to work alongside my family on our farm. It makes me realize how important it is to be an advocate for agriculture. A lot of people think that agriculture is "just farming," but it includes everything from nurturing the soil to harvesting crops to raising animals. I'm learning responsibility, teamwork, and community spirit, all while spending time with my family.

Before I get on my school bus in the morning, I let the cows and their calves out of the barn and check with my dad to see if he needs help with any chores. When I get home from school in the afternoon, I begin a variety of farm chores, including rounding up and feeding our six horses; feeding, giving water to, and gathering eggs from our chickens; giving

My sister Kate and I, brushing our 4-H projects. It is a long
process to get the calves quieted down, and this is how it starts.

My "trusty steed" Max and our family dog Heidi. I have had
Max since I was 5. He is such an awesome guy!

Riding Max while bringing cattle home from summer pasture

water to our pigs; and putting out grain in the yearling pen. (A yearling is a calf that is 1 to 2 years old.) There are sometimes more or different chores to do depending on the season, like in early spring when our cows give birth. I help to tag the newborn calves.

My parents have jobs off the farm, so it is very important for my sister and me to pitch in. My dad always says, "Teamwork gets the job done faster." He and I undertake a lot of tasks together, like fencing and working in the garden. As a foursome, our family tackles many chores, such as yard work and—nobody's favorite—cleaning the chicken barn. These jobs take less time with more than one person doing them, and it is definitely more fun when you have someone to talk with while you work.

My favorite thing to do on the farm is to work with the cattle. Every year, I train a steer for showing at the 4-H fair. I train him to lead (which means to willingly walk with me while he is on a lead) and tie up in a "show stance" (which means to stop and pose for the judges). Training cattle makes them easier to work with, but it takes a lot of time and patience. I enjoy every minute of it!

As a member of the local 4-H club, I am very active in and around our community. The organization encourages us to promote community spirit and help people in need—this could be anything from helping to fix farm equipment to moving cattle to preparing a meal for someone who is very busy.

I love agriculture, and I want to stay involved with it throughout my life and especially in my career. I feel fortunate to have the privileges and opportunities that come with being part of a family farm.

Clockwise from above left: Kate and I started helping on the farm at a young age. In these photos of us, at ages 4 and 7, we are helping our dad move cattle, operating the rear gate for the cattle-handling chute, and petting my first 4-H project, Pepper. A local family gave me Pepper on the day he was born.

You see vegetables at markets and on your plate, but do you know how they got their start?

IN THE GARDEN

ASPARAGUS

Asparagus spears usually sprout from a crown. This is a cluster of small buds surrounded by long, stringy roots.

A crown is planted in a trench of soil. A mound is made in the trench and the roots are spread over it. Then the crown and roots are covered with a few inches of soil. As the buds grow into tall spears, more soil is added around the spears. Asparagus spears can grow up to 6 inches per day, and the roots can grow to be 5 to 6 feet long! The spears can be green, white, or purple.

Asparagus is not harvested until the second or third year after being planted. This allows the plant to become strong.

In summer, the spears turn into tall, feathery ferns that produce food for the crown. If the ferns are cut down before they wilt, the crown will not produce healthy spears in the next year.

Did you know? Ancient Romans enjoyed asparagus so much that emperors dispatched fleets to find and transport the best spears to Rome.

BEETS

Beets grow from chunky, light brown seeds. Usually, one seed can produce two or three seedlings.

Beet seeds are planted in fertile, soft soil that is free of rocks, stones, and clumps of dirt. If the soil is rocky or clumpy, the beet roots will not grow properly.

Beets produce green and reddish leaves above ground and spherical roots below ground. The roots can be dark red, yellow, or white. Some are even red and white–striped inside!

Beets are harvested when the roots poke up through the soil and are about the size of a golf ball or softball. Both beet leaves and roots can be eaten.

Did you know? The juice of red beets can stain your fingers. To remove the coloring, rub with lemon juice.

BRUSSELS SPROUTS

Brussels sprouts' dark brown seeds form in pods and are about the size of peppercorns.

The plant's stem develops into a thick stalk. Leaves grow out of the stem and top. The sprouts begin as tiny, round balls in the leaves' axils (where the leaves grow out of the stem). A full-size brussels sprouts plant looks similar to a small palm tree.

The sprouts are picked from the bottom up, when they are as small as a nickel or as large as an egg. Ripe sprouts come off the stalk easily when twisted.

Brussels sprouts grow best in cool seasons—even winter. Frost or snow improves their flavor.

Did you know?

In nature, brussels sprouts pods burst to release seeds. Gardeners can release seeds by rubbing the pods between the palms of their hands or putting the pods into a bag and jumping on it.

Did you know?

Some baby carrots in grocery stores are actually full-size carrots that have been cut and "polished" smooth. True baby carrots are grown to have a fat top and pointed end like full-size varieties.

CARROTS

Carrot seeds are tiny, yet they produce vegetables that are 7 inches long, on average.

Carrots grow best in deep, sandy soil. If the soil is firm or rocky, the roots will not grow straight. The seeds are planted close together. When the green, feathery tops are about 3 inches high, some are pulled out (called "thinning") so that the remaining carrots have room to grow.

Carrot roots can be orange, red, purple, yellow, or white. Carrots are ready to harvest when the roots poke up through the soil.

CUCUMBERS

Most cucumber seeds are about the size of a grain of rice.

They are planted in fertile soil, several feet apart. Cucumbers need a lot of water. There are two types of cucumber plants—vining cucumbers and bush cucumbers. Both types produce fast-growing vines with hairy stems. Vining cucumbers grow along the ground unless a trellis or fence is available for them to grow up. Bush varieties are sturdy, shrublike plants that take up a lot less space.

Cucumber plants produce large flowers. When the petals wither, the cucumbers begin to grow.

If ripe cucumbers are not picked, the plant will stop producing until the vegetables are removed.

Did you know? Cucumbers can be grown in clear plastic molds that turn them into shapes like stars and hearts!

Did you know? The word "lettuce" comes from words meaning "milky" and describes the white sap (latex) that the vegetable can produce.

LETTUCE

Lettuce seeds are tiny, flat, and oval. They will grow almost anywhere, except in hot temperatures. Lettuce likes loose soil that drains well.

Lettuce can form in heads, leaves, or loaf shapes (such as romaine) and can be green, red, or purple. Some leaf varieties are even speckled! Leaf lettuce grows relatively quickly—in about 45 to 50 days.

Lettuce heads are harvested one head at a time. Leaf lettuce is harvested one leaf (or several) at a time. This is why leaf lettuce is sometimes called "cut-and-come-again" lettuce.

PEAS

Pea seeds, which are dried peas, can be smooth or wrinkled. Wrinkled ones produce sweeter peas. Peas like fertile, sandy soil. Soil with too much nitrogen will produce leafy plants but few pea pods.

Pea seeds send up vines that can grow from 2 to 6 feet tall and produce tendrils (thin, threadlike stems). These tiny stems then reach out to supports such as thin tree branches, string placed between stakes, or fencing.

Pea plants produce small, white flowers. Pea pods appear after the petals wither.

There are three types of peas: Snow peas produce pods that are flat, with tiny peas inside. They are eaten raw or cooked in the pod. Snap peas produce fat pods with large peas packed tightly inside. These are eaten raw or cooked in the pod. Garden peas produce pods with large peas inside that are removed from the pod to be eaten raw or cooked.

Did you know?
Peas were a bedtime snack for royalty in 17th-century France.

Did you know?
You can soothe a sunburn using a potato. Grate a peeled potato, then spread gratings on the burn, which the potato's starch will cool and soothe.

POTATOES

Potato plants grow from seed potatoes, which are small potatoes that have been grown specifically to be replanted. Seed potatoes sprout buds called "eyes." A seed potato with at least two eyes is ready to plant.

A seed potato is planted, eyes facing up, in a trench made in fertile, sandy soil. Then it is covered with a few inches of soil. Once stems and leaves emerge, more soil is added, until a small hill is formed. The plant turns into a small bush and flowers bloom on it.

When the flowers and leaves die, the potatoes are ready to be dug up. Potatoes can be brown, yellow, red, blue, or purple.

Sow-Easy Seed Balls

IF YOU CAN THROW, YOU CAN GROW!

Rolling Through History

- Ancient Egyptians used seed balls to restore plantings after the Nile River's annual spring flood.
- Native American tribes transported their seeds in seed balls as they moved from place to place.
- Seed balls were made popular in 1938 by Japanese farmer and philosopher Masanobu Fukuoka. He called seed balls *tsuchi dango,* or Earth dumplings.

Want to have some fun while making the world a greener, more beautiful place? Make seed balls! A technique for distributing seeds without tilling or digging in the ground, seed balls are commonly used to enrich bare, desolate, or hard-to-cultivate areas. Also known as seed bombs, these little nuggets are made up of clay, compost, and seeds. They do not have to be planted in a hole—instead, they can be dropped directly on the ground. Even better, you can throw seed balls and let the seeds grow wherever they land!

Because seed ball seeds are encased in a mixture of clay and compost, they are nourished and protected from drying out in the sun, getting blown way, or being eaten by animals. The seed balls have everything that they need to grow, except water. You can wait for Mother Nature to do this chore or water them yourself. When the water softens the clay coating, the seeds inside start to sprout. As the seedlings grow, the coating breaks down and the roots reach down into the ground. This simple method is easy, entertaining, and environmentally friendly.

Note: Do not throw seed balls into other people's yards or public areas (such as parks) without permission!

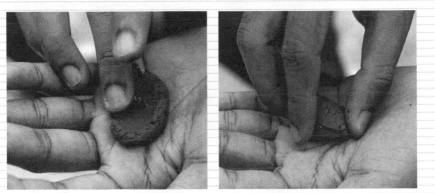

HOW TO MAKE SEED BALLS

YOU WILL NEED:

baking sheet	powdered clay	flower seeds (see below)
wax paper	compost or potting soil	empty egg carton
bucket	water	

1. Line the baking sheet with wax paper.

2. In the bucket, mix 2 cups of clay with 1 cup of compost.

3. Add a little water so that the mixture is moist but not soaking wet. It should be the consistency of cookie dough.

4. Pinch off a small amount of the mixture (enough to make balls slightly smaller than a golf ball) and press three to five seeds into it.

5. Roll into a ball and place on the lined cookie sheet.

6. Repeat, making more of the clay/compost mixture as needed for the amount of seeds that you have.

7. Allow the seed balls to dry outside in a shady area for 24 to 48 hours.

8. Store your seed balls in an empty egg carton until it is time to ready, aim, flower!

Need Seeds?

Good choices for seed balls include:

Aster	Clover	Cosmos	Marigold	Poppy
Black-eyed Susan	Cornflower	Goldenrod	Milkweed	Sunflower
		Lobelia		Yarrow

Also, you can ask a local nursery which wildflowers are native to your area and make a mixed seed ball from the suggestions. Try to use seeds of similar size in each ball.

NATURE'S

Mother Nature sure knows how to have a good time!
All of the plants on these pages—and more
on the next several pages—seem to have been
specially designed, created, and named
for us as symbols of holidays and happenings.
Turn the page now to see and celebrate!

PARTY PLANTS

HAPPY BIRTHDAY!
NOW, MAKE A WISH!

'Royal Candles', a variety of speedwell, "light up" with purplish-blue spikes covered with tiny flowers in early spring and summer—and they can't be blown out! This plant needs rich soil, lots of sun, and regular watering, especially when young. With care, 'Royal Candles' will grow back every year.

Feast your eyes on 'Ice Cream' tulips! Imagine vanilla ice cream in a red berry "cone" growing out of the ground. How about Strawberry Ice Cream in a green "bowl"? While these flowers are not edible, they also don't melt! Here's the scoop: Plant these rare tulips in a sunny location in autumn so that they'll bloom in spring.

VALENTINE'S DAY
HAVE A HEART—OR A FEW!

The pillow-y, pink-and-white blooms of bleeding heart dangle on thin stems and quiver in a light breeze—almost as if beating! Show this classic beauty some love with rich, moist soil; shade from the sun; and regular watering.

Hearts-a-bustin' blooms are not broken—they only look like they are. This bush's 1-inch-wide, bumpy flower "capsules" split open when they are ripe (in autumn) to reveal four or five orange-red seeds. This plant prefers shade and slightly acidic, well-draining soil.

ST. PATRICK'S DAY
GO GREEN!

The foliage of cloverlike oxalis, or flowering shamrock, is loaded with lucky charm! Before opening, the blooms look like closed umbrellas. The plant's little bulbs resemble pinecones or dry sticks but thrive in gritty soil, filtered light, and modest moisture indoors. Outside, give it rich soil, lots of sun, and regular watering.

EASTER
NO YOKE!

The fruit of the 'Easter Egg' eggplant will crack you up. This 12-inch-tall plant produces purple flowers in late spring, followed by a dozen ornamental (nonedible) white "eggs" that would fool any Chicken Little. As the eggs age, they turn orange. Grow it from seed in rich soil and sun, with regular watering.

Convert to metric on p. 187

fountain grass

goldenrod

amaranth

FOURTH OF JULY
SIZZLERS AND SPARKLERS

Not all fireworks light up the sky; some are at your feet. The pink and red foliage of clumpy 'Fireworks' fountain grass almost sparkles, while the bright pink, yellow-tip blooms of 'Fireworks' amaranth seem to explode. Bushy 'Fireworks' goldenrod shows off its 18-inch,

STAR LIGHT, STAR BRIGHT
OUT OF THIS WORLD!

As surely as the Perseid meteor showers light up the night sky from August 11 to 13, 'Night Sky' petunia will brighten the daytime. Its purple petals are speckled with almost as many stars as twinkle in the heavens. Each bloom displays a different pattern, and all are affected by temperature. Hot days and cool nights bring out the white spots; hot days and nights tend to bring out more purple. This one-of-a-kind annual grows in full sun and should be watered regularly.

tumbleweed onion

brilliant yellow flower spikes like skyrockets.

'Alcazar' red-hot poker looks almost too hot to touch: Its flamelike flowers blaze yellow, orange, and red on stems as tall as 4 feet!

Tumbleweed onion produces flower heads loaded with purplish, spidery flowers resembling a beautiful explosion.

This celebratory collection likes rich soil, sun, and regular watering.

red-hot poker

HALLOWEEN
HAPPY HAUNTING!

There's a fungus among us! *Xylaria polymorpha,* aka dead man's fingers, looks like clusters of 1½- to 4-inch-tall human fingers or even hand-shape forms—flesh-color or black, sometimes with the appearance of fingernails! It grows on wood, especially buried hardwood and decaying tree stumps.

Eek! Blood! When the bright-red root of the bloodroot plant is cut open, it "bleeds" red-orange sap. This liquid, used as a dye by Native Americans, may leave a stain on skin and clothing and could be poisonous if ingested. Look for bloodroot in early spring in forests and along streams. Its white, daisylike flowers open in sunlight and close at night.

Trick or treat? Now you see it, now you don't: In dry weather, the skeleton flower bears umbrella-shape white blooms, but when the petals are touched by rain, they magically become clear like glass! As they dry, they turn white again. This plant prefers rich soil and a shady spot.

THANKSGIVING
LET US GIVE THANKS

We are not the only ones who feast on some sort of turkey: Every winter, thousands of animals and insects dine on the acorns or leaves of the American turkey oak tree. So named because its leaves resemble a turkey foot or track, the American turkey oak is native to the U.S. South and thrives in dry, sandy areas, reaching as tall as 100 feet. Squirrels, deer, rabbits, raccoons, wood ducks, and other critters like the taste of its acorns; birds eat up the insects in and on it. (Cattle, goats, and sheep should be kept away; the turkey oak could be poisonous to them.)

Would you know a turkey tail fungus if you saw one in the woods? Commonly found on dead or rotting stumps, it displays tan to brown layers that resemble a turkey's tail feathers. Although often called a "mushroom," it is a polypore (with pores instead of gills) consisting of layers (it has no stalk and cap) that can thrive for weeks ("mushrooms" normally last only hours or days).

Grow a
FIRST AID KIT

Explore the benefits of aloe vera.

Ancient Egyptians called it the "plant of immortality" and early Native American tribes called it "wand of heaven," but we call it aloe vera. Originally grown in southern Africa, aloe vera is a succulent, which is a plant that has thick, fleshy leaves that store water. Its leaves are also full of healing substances that have been used medicinally for at least 6,000 years.

Aloe plants produce two things: gel and latex. The clear gel is in the pointed leaves. The latex is yellow and found just under the plant's green skin. Both the gel and the latex have healing properties.

How to GROW ALOE

Aloe vera is an easy-to-grow houseplant. It can survive outside, but only in frost-free areas. Aloe plants continually send out from their roots new shoots called "pups," which you can pull up and replant. If you know anyone with a thriving aloe plant, ask them to pull out a pup for you. Plant it in good potting soil (soil made for cacti is perfect) and set it in a sunny spot. Water your plant about every 3 weeks and even less during winter. Push your finger into the soil to test for dryness. You want the soil to dry at least 1 to 2 inches deep before watering.

Leaf for RELIEF

Using the leaf straight from the plant is the best way to get aloe's healing properties. The gel can help to heal and ease the pain of burns, bruises, boils, canker sores, and chapped lips. It may also lessen symptoms of acne. For aloe relief:

• Remove one of the swordlike leaves from a living plant and open it along its length. Then either squeeze out the gel and apply it where relief is needed or lay the entire opened leaf side directly over the affected area and then bandage it lightly in place.

• Remove a leaf from an aloe plant. Cut open the leaf and use a spoon to scrape out the clear gel. Put the gel pieces into a blender and pulse several times, until the aloe is liquid. Pour the gel into clean ice cube trays and place in the freezer.

Once the aloe has frozen, pop the cubes out of the ice cube tray and store them in a zipper-lock bag back in the freezer. Label the bag so that no one puts your aloe cubes in their drink!

To use, remove an aloe cube and apply to sunburned skin, bug bites, poison ivy rash, or any other ailment that requires relief.

Try a small amount of aloe on a patch of skin; if you notice a rash, swelling, or itching, do not use.

Aloe for HAIR AND SKIN

To condition hair and leave it healthy-looking and shiny, scrape some gel out of the leaves and massage it into your hair. Wait for about 5 minutes, then rinse it out with warm or cold water.

To use aloe as a skin moisturizer, just scoop out the gel or rub a freshly cut leaf over your skin and let it dry.

DID YOU KNOW?

As humans build more houses and towns in wilderness areas, some wild animals have discovered that city life suits them. Scientists have suggested that a new field may be needed to study the resulting conflicts: anthrotherology, combining the Greek words for human *(anthropos)* and wild animal *(ther)*.

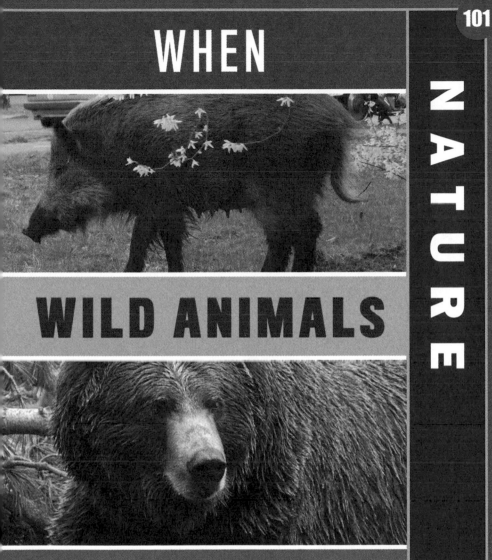

WHEN

WILD ANIMALS

COME TO TOWN

Anytime wild animals and people cross
paths, the results can be surprising, comical—
or even distressing and dangerous.

GOT HONEY?

Tina Aucker got the surprise of her life when she greeted an unusual customer at Aunt Mahalia's Candies in Gatlinburg, Tennessee. Inside the store was a big black bear. Tina stared, then politely said, "Hang on one moment, and I'll be right back." As soon as she turned to yell to a coworker, the bear left, leaving behind a large paw print on a rug.

Encounters like this one are common in bear country. From Tennessee to Alaska, bears knock over trash cans, break into cars, and sometimes even climb through kitchen windows, all in search of food. Officials warn people in such areas to beware—black bears can eat up to 20,000 calories a day when they're getting ready to hibernate. As a result, some cities and towns require residents to use bearproof trash cans.

But bears can be sneaky: Security cameras caught one bruin stealing treats from a candy store in Estes Park, Colorado. Early one July morning, before the store was open, the bear nudged open the door and eventually made seven round-trips during 20 minutes of gooey grabbing. The animal snatched candy as well as the store's special cookie bears, taking them outside to enjoy. "He was very clean and careful," the store owner reported.

GO, MONKEY, GO!

Twenty-five pounds of trouble—that's one way to describe a rhesus macaque (REE-sus ma-COCK) monkey that eluded captors in Tampa, Florida, for more than 3 years. No one knew exactly where the monkey came from, but it was believed that he had been forced out of a colony of wild monkeys that was living beside a river about 100 miles away.

No matter how hard they tried, trappers couldn't catch the monkey as it swung from neighborhood tree to tree, poked through store dumpsters, and traveled around three counties. Wildlife officials tried tempting him with roast beef sandwiches, apples, and candy bars. The clever monkey either stayed hidden or took the bait and ran.

Someone created a Facebook page for "Mystery Monkey," and fans cheered "Go, monkey, go!" He had many adventures, including playing on top of a church roof during a service and swinging out of trees and into family swimming pools. Frustrated wildlife officials named him Cornelius, after a character from the science fiction classic *Planet of the Apes.*

For about 2 years, Cornelius seemed to have settled in a neighborhood in St. Petersburg, where residents frequently left fruit out to feed him. One day, however, he jumped on a woman's back and bit her shoulder. After a 5-hour stakeout, wildlife officials were able to trap Cornelius. One of his captors said, "This is one of the most intelligent monkeys that I think I have ever seen."

Cornelius now lives in a Florida zoo, where he has become a father.

MOOSE ON THE LOOSE

Visitors come and go at Alaska Regional Hospital in Anchorage, but nobody was expecting the moose that came through the automatic doors into a hospital hallway. In 2005, a camera recorded the animal as it looked around and then turned and left. Eleven years later, another moose came for a visit—and this one hung around for 3 days! It spent most of its time in the parking garage, wandering all the way up to the third floor. The animal went inside briefly, through a set of automatic doors. Throughout the weekend, security guards kept an eye on the moose to make sure that the animal and everyone around it stayed safe.

Anchorage is famous for its moose, and with around 1,500 of them living in and around the city, they're easy to see. The city's Web site boasts that tourists may spot one in the first hour of their visit. Moose in Anchorage regularly cause traffic jams or get their antlers tangled in things like Christmas lights, ziplines, and swing sets. One moose gave birth in the parking lot of a hardware store. When the calf took its first steps, people cheered.

Sometimes residents have to wait for a moose to move before they can leave their driveways or walk in their front door. Anchorage police often use their patrol cars to escort moose out of harm's way, with their lights and sirens blaring. "They come through the yard all the time," one Alaskan explained, "and sometimes they take their naps back there."

MOSCOW'S CANINE COMMUTERS

A train pulls into a subway station in Moscow, its doors open, and a large black dog boards. He hops onto a seat and stretches, taking up two spots next to a man reading a newspaper. A few stops later, this four-legged rider hops down from his perch and leaves the train. Canine commuters like this one aren't unusual in Moscow, where 30,000 or more stray dogs roam Russia's capital. About 500 live at subway stops, which are particularly inviting during the city's cold winters. Some have learned to ride the trains.

Biologist Andrei Poyarkov has studied these dogs for decades, often following them as they ride. He says that some take short rides from time to time, while others spend their days riding back and forth, begging passengers for food and affection. These savvy commuters can even figure out where they are by recognizing smells and the announcements made at different stations. All that, and these subway dogs don't even need a ticket!

BEWARE OF BABOON BURGLARS

The Happy Valley homeless shelter near Cape Town, South Africa, prides itself on feeding hungry visitors—except for bothersome baboons. "They know what time we serve food," one worker said. "Usually they come right before lunch."

Baboons are a big problem in certain areas of Cape Town, whose mountains are home to large groups of these animals, called "troops." "Where there's a mountain, there's a baboon," noted one Cape Town researcher. "As we take up more and more of their land, the conflict increases." They prowl through the city, raiding trash bins, markets, and homes, flashing their sharp teeth at anyone who tries to stop them. In addition to food, they've been known to steal things like curtains, keys, and even teddy bears. City employees try to scare them away with flares, pepper spray, and paintball guns. (It's illegal to feed, kill, or hurt baboons in Cape Town.)

One 12-year-old boy had a terrifying encounter with a troop that had broken into his home. When he confronted them as they tore apart his family's kitchen, three males chased him upstairs. As he called for help, the baboons surrounded him and began bombarding him with fruit.

Scientists have studied the animals' tactics with the help of tracking collars that monitor their movements. The animals also intrigue tourists, who often feed them to get a closer view, despite numerous signs warning them otherwise. Some baboons—especially the leaders of troops, "alpha males"—are bold enough to snatch food right out of people's hands. Stopping such raids is tricky; conservationists warn that removing the males hurts the baboon population.

FLORIDA'S UNWELCOME TOURISTS

A family in Miami, Florida, woke up to an unexpected visitor one Christmas morning, and it wasn't Santa Claus. Instead, they found a 13-foot-long Burmese python curled up in the corner of their swimming pool. After their 9-1-1 call, a special fire department team trained to capture snakes and other potentially dangerous creatures arrived to remove the uninvited guest.

Florida has a big problem with pythons, one of the largest snakes in the world. Although these snakes are native to Asia, not Florida, people have brought them to the Sunshine State. Some pythons escaped into the wild; others were released by pet owners who got tired of caring for them. Perhaps they didn't realize that those baby snakes would grow to be 16 to 23 feet long and weigh 200 pounds!

Although pythons aren't poisonous, they bite, and they can wrap themselves around animals (and occasionally people) and squeeze until their victim suffocates. They target Florida's native species, such as marsh rabbits and wading birds, and also rob native predators like panthers and alligators of food sources. The state created the Python Elimination Program to reduce the number of pythons, and it seems to be working: More than 1,000 have been eliminated, including one 132-pound specimen over 17 feet long!

BOAR WARS IN BERLIN

Berlin, Germany, has become the "wild boar capital of the world." Forests cover 20 percent of the city, making it an inviting habitat. Around 7,000 of these hogs call Berlin home; they dig up gardens, cause road accidents, and terrorize neighborhoods. "We receive calls [about them] every day," said one environmental group worker.

Joggers and dog walkers are accustomed to encountering the boars. Although these pigs are typically shy around people, they can become aggressive when cornered or injured and have occasionally attacked. When they do, watch out! Weighing as much as 400 pounds, wild boars have sharp tusks and can charge at speeds of up to 31 miles per hour!

A wandering herd once forced a train to stop. One unfortunate boar got stuck inside a telephone booth. Five boars broke through a fence and tore up a field belonging to Berlin's men's soccer team. Two days later, after the fence had been fixed, the boars broke through again. Another group of boars uprooted graves at a cemetery, causing more than $14,000 in damage.

The Panda Puzzler

I s the giant panda a bear or a raccoon? Pandas, although bearlike in looks and the way they walk, are unlike bears in many ways: They have six (instead of five) toes on their front feet, they have distinct black and white markings, they are vegetarians, and they do not hibernate. Pandas don't even roar like bears—they bleat, like sheep!

In 1869, a Catholic priest stationed in China became the first westerner to see a giant panda. He sent a letter to a mammal expert at the Paris Museum of Natural History describing his find. He proposed the Latin name *Ursus melanoleucus,* meaning "black and white bear." Later, after the mammalogist had examined the remains of a giant panda, he decided that it was more similar to members of the raccoon family and reclassified it as *Ailuropoda melanoleuca,* meaning "black and white cat foot."

It wasn't until decades later—when DNA technology became available—that we got the final answer to the question of how to classify the panda. The results showed that giant pandas' closest relatives are . . . bears!

Mosses *and* Liverworts *and* Lichens— Oh, My!

The next time you go for a walk in the woods, look beyond the trees: Some of the most fascinating living organisms are right beneath your feet! Mosses, liverworts, and lichens may be small, but they are a big part of our natural world.

MOSS

There are about 10,000 species of mosses in the world today. Mosses first appeared on Earth 350 million years ago. Dinosaurs weren't even alive at that time!

Mosses do not have woody stems and most therefore can not grow large. Most are usually no more than 1 inch tall. The one exception is *Dawsonia*, the world's tallest moss. Extra cells on its leaves allow it to grow to be 24 inches tall!

Mosses can be found on all continents, including the world's coldest, Antarctica. To stay warm there, mosses soak up sunlight.

Mosses grow in groups, creating what can look like a big green carpet. They don't have seeds or flowers, so they spread by spores. Spores can be carried by the wind to nearby areas, where they land and begin to grow.

Mosses are coated in wax. This helps them to retain water and keep it from evaporating. They don't like hot, dry areas, which is why you usually find them in damp, shady spots. Mosses can not live in salt water; they need fresh water to survive.

Large mats of mosses can help to slow down the rush of water when it rains, preventing a flood. Other plants that need lots of water to survive like to grow near mosses, so that they can share the water and nutrients trapped by mosses. Insects, grubs, and small animals such as salamanders and frogs make their homes in mosses.

Some mosses form bogs that produce peat. Peat is a soil-like substance that can be used as a source of fuel in some parts of the world. Because peat can hold a lot of water, it is often added to garden soil so that the plants do not have to be watered too often.

During World War I, a type of moss called "sphagnum" was collected and used with gauze bandages to treat soldiers' wounds. Sphagnum has antiseptic properties, so it helped to prevent infection and to stop bleeding.

LIVERWORT

Liverworts are tiny. Some are so small that you need a magnifying glass to see them!

Liverwort's name comes from its shape. Hundreds of years ago, herbalists thought that some of the plants resembled a liver and used it to treat liver ailments. The word *wort* means "small plant."

Liverworts were living on Earth at least 400 million years ago. They are even older than mosses.

It is estimated that there are 8,000 species of liverworts worldwide. Most live in cool, moist, shady areas, such as under rocks or logs. Some can live even on the surface of freshwater ponds and lakes.

Liverworts don't have roots. They have cells that attach to the ground. These cells help them to spread along the ground to form mats. Liverworts can also reproduce by making spores, which serve as seeds.

Liverworts do not have leaves. Instead, they have little scales that sit on top of tiny, thin stems.

Liverworts make slime that helps them to absorb water. When liverworts do not receive enough water, the scales dry out and the plants stop growing until they get water again.

LICHEN

Have you ever seen a growth on a rock or tree? It was probably a lichen! Lichens look a little like mosses and liverworts, but they are not plants. They can be bright orange, yellow, green, white, or even black in color. It is believed that there are 25,000 different species of lichens on Earth.

Lichens are formed from a combination of fungi and algae or bacteria, or both. On their own, algae or bacteria can not live in harsh climates, but if they combine with fungi, they can survive. That's why lichens are found all over the world. They can live in hot, dry areas and in extreme cold. Some lichens can live even near the sea.

Although they are not plants, lichens make food in the same way as plants by using energy from the Sun. They reproduce using special cells that help them to spread.

Lichens can absorb water from the air as well as from the ground. Like liverworts, lichens dry up when they do not have enough water. When they rehydrate, they "wake up" and start to make food again.

Lichens can absorb pollutants from the air. Scientists study lichen populations to try to understand how much pollution is in an area. They take tissue samples from lichens and measure the amount of pollution that has been absorbed.

Lichens are an important food source for some species of crabs, snails, and slugs, as well as insects such as caterpillars and grasshoppers. In the Arctic, reindeer and caribou feed on lichen during the long, cold winters. A single caribou or reindeer can eat between 6 and 11 pounds of lichen every day!

Our Regal Eagle

The bald eagle is an extraordinary bird. One of the largest eagles in North America, it is 30 to 43 inches tall with a wingspan 6 to 8 feet wide from the tip of one wing to the tip of the other. The most noticeable feature is its head. Don't be fooled by its name—this bird isn't bald. Instead, an adult bald eagle's head is covered in bright white feathers. (An older meaning of "bald" was "white-headed.") Its body is chocolate brown, with a white, wedge-shape tail and yellow eyes, legs, and feet. Females are slightly larger than males. Young eagles are all brown—from head to tail to eyes to beak. As they age, their feathers become spotted with white and their eyes and beak turn yellow. By age 5, they are adults.

Convert to metric on p. 187

DID YOU KNOW?
Adult bald eagles have about 7,000 feathers.

The bald eagle is a raptor, a bird that feeds mainly on meat. These eagles love to eat fish and will steal a fresh catch from another bird or animal. They also eat dead animals or garbage. Reptiles, amphibians, small mammals, and birds are all on the menu. Bald eagles' eyes can see a meal more than a mile away! The birds perch on high branches to look for prey or cruise along water surfaces, scanning what lies beneath. Their sharp claws (called "talons") are perfect for grabbing prey out of the water. If a fish is too heavy to lift, a bald eagle can use its wings to paddle its way to shore while still holding on to its dinner.

1.　2.　3.　4.

NATIONAL BIRDS

The bald eagle is the national bird of the United States. Other countries have also selected eagles as their national birds. Can you match each country with its emblem?

1. African fish eagle	a. Germany
2. Golden eagle	b. Indonesia
3. Harpy eagle	c. Namibia
4. Javan hawk-eagle	d. Panama

Answers: 1. c; 2. a; 3. d; 4. b

In the wild, bald eagles live 15 to 28 years. They are found mostly in Canada and Alaska but can be spotted as far south as northern Mexico. These birds stay near bodies of water where they can fish. Although often alone, they sometimes hang out in large groups. Some stay all year in one place, while others move to areas that offer lots of food for the winter.

ALL-AMERICAN EAGLE

After the signing of the Declaration of Independence in 1776, Congress was looking for a symbol for the Great Seal of the United States. Charles Thomson came up with the winning design—the front of the seal showed a bald eagle—and the United States had its national bird.

IN FULL RECOVERY

In 1967, bald eagles were listed as endangered in many areas. After conservation efforts, they recovered. In 1995, the birds were changed to being in "threatened" status, before being removed from the federal government's endangered list in 2007.

Convert to metric on p. 187

DID YOU KNOW?

The largest known bald eagle nest was found near St. Petersburg, Florida. It was 9½ feet wide, 20 feet deep, and estimated to weigh 4,409 pounds.

The nests of bald eagles are made of woven sticks and lined with lichen, moss, grasses, down, and other soft materials. They can be found in tall evergreens, on cliffs, on the ground, or even on top of cacti or phone towers. Bald eagles make some of the largest bird nests in the world. An average bald eagle nest is 2 to 4 feet tall and 5 to 6 feet wide. These enormous nests take up to 3 months to build.

SPECIAL SIGNIFICANCE

Some Native American tribes believe that the bald eagle is sacred. To them, the bird symbolizes bravery, honor, wisdom, strength, healing, love, or spiritual guidance.

When it is time to lay eggs in the nest, the male and female bald eagle will defend their area. They chase off predators and any other raptors that try to build a nest within a mile or two of their own. The female will lay one to four off-white eggs, each about 3 inches long and 2 inches wide. The parents take turns sitting on the eggs until they hatch, which takes about 35 days. After the fluffy, grayish white chicks appear, the mother stays with them while the father hunts for food. After about 3 months, the young birds' feathers are strong enough to enable their first flight. For several weeks, they will take short flights, getting ready to leave the nest.

Bald eagles can fly as fast as 30 miles per hour but can dive at up to 100 mph. In one day, adults may fly 50 to 125 miles. They often soar, holding their wings open and catching rising air underneath them. This is less work than constantly flapping wings. These birds can fly more than 10,000 feet high!

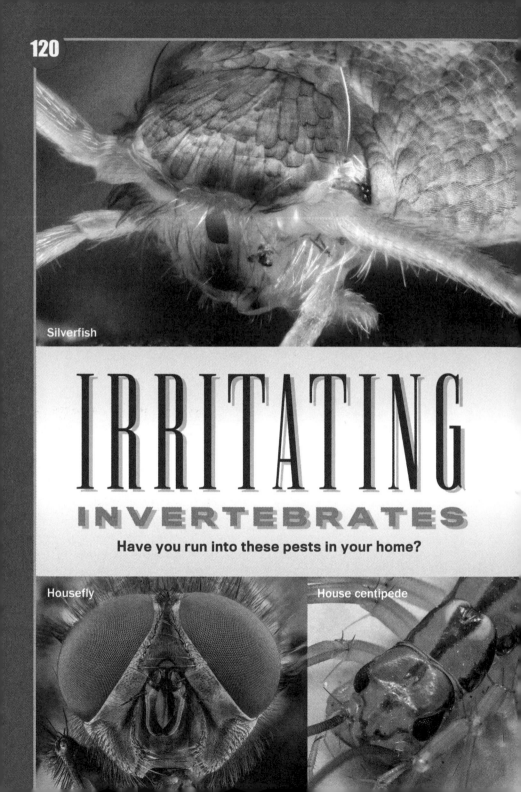

Silverfish

IRRITATING
INVERTEBRATES
Have you run into these pests in your home?

Housefly

House centipede

DARK DWELLER

I t's the middle of the night, and you're sleepily stumbling toward the bathroom in the dark. You flip the light switch and see a sudden movement at your feet. You look down, only to see a tiny, silver-color, lightning-fast critter skitter away into a dark corner of the room—*Eek!* What *is* that?

This mysterious creature is nothing more than a harmless household pest: the **silverfish.**

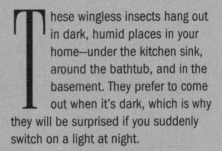

T hese wingless insects hang out in dark, humid places in your home—under the kitchen sink, around the bathtub, and in the basement. They prefer to come out when it's dark, which is why they will be surprised if you suddenly switch on a light at night.

F or a pest, the silverfish has a pretty cool name. Its silver-gray scales resemble those of a fish, and the side-to-side motion that it makes when it scurries away looks like that of a fish swimming upstream. The silverfish usually gets no longer than ½ inch and has several appendages protruding from its front and rear. Its six stubby legs allow the silverfish to move at incredible speeds and escape potential predators (like you).

Silverfish do not bite or attack humans; instead, they feed on materials such as bookbinding and wallpaper glue, dry foods in your kitchen pantry, and nonsynthetic cloth. Because of this, they can be rather destructive pests when they appear in large numbers.

DID YOU KNOW?

When looking for a mate, silverfish perform a complex, three-part dance consisting of antenna-wagging, playful chasing, and abdomen-shaking. The routine may last more than half an hour!

CREEPY CRAWLER

Commonly known as "hundred-leggers," **house centipedes** rank among the creepiest household pests around. With their long, spindly legs and quick movements, they're able to strike fear into the heart of anyone who stumbles across them.

However, house centipedes are not the worst pest to have in your home. In fact, they actually prey upon more problematic pests, such as cockroaches, carpet beetles, and silverfish. That's right—they're one of the good guys!

An effective predator, the house centipede has 15 pairs of long, thin legs that help it to climb most surfaces with ease. It has a venomous sting that easily immobilizes prey but causes only slight pain and irritation in humans, who are very rarely stung (and usually only when a centipede is truly pestered).

DID YOU KNOW?

The house centipede came from the Mediterranean region of Europe but has been spread throughout the world by humans. Man-made structures provide the perfect winter habitat to protect house centipedes from the cold.

House centipedes typically live in damp, dark places, such as under the sink or in the basement, but occasionally you will find this multilegged creepy-crawly hanging out *in* your sink or bathtub. House centipedes are attracted to the moisture in these areas at night, but once they fall in, the smooth surfaces prevent them from crawling out, leaving them trapped. If this happens, resist the urge to squish this pest and just release it outside instead.

NAGGING NUISANCE

Have you ever been pestered by a housefly that just won't go away? Well, you're not alone. The **housefly** is a super-common insect pest that's found all over the world. They are well known for being determined in their pursuit of food, but then again, you would be, too, if you lived for only about 3 weeks!

For a housefly, a trash can is like an all-you-can-eat buffet. They love the smell of old, rotting food—especially vegetables, fruit, and meat, as well as human and animal waste. All of the things that we find absolutely disgusting, houseflies find positively delicious.

Houseflies may be annoying, but unlike some other types of flies, houseflies do not bite—in fact, they *can't* bite. A housefly doesn't have teeth, and its mouth is designed to suck up liquids like a sponge does. This is why the housefly prefers to eat food that's already starting to go bad—it's essentially pre-chewed! Houseflies don't have tongues; they taste their meals with tiny hairs on their feet, which explains why they always seem so intent on crawling over every inch of your food. (They often stop to rub their feet together, in part to clean their receptors.)

Although houseflies are mostly just bothersome and gross, they aren't totally harmless. Because they eat only liquid foods, houseflies are constantly sucking up and spitting out bacteria, viruses, and other microorganisms along with their meals. This means that they can sometimes spread nasty diseases to humans, so keep them away from your food as best as you can and wash your hands if you touch any flies.

DID YOU KNOW?

Shoo-fly pie, a tasty Amish dessert from the 1700s, is said to be so named because its sweet and gooey molasses filling is highly attractive to flies. This made it necessary for colonial bakers to keep a close eye on their creations and occasionally exclaim "Shoo, fly!" to scare the pests away.

Uncommon Kids

You're never too young to make a difference in the world, as these accomplished kids demonstrate.

The Nutrition Expert

When she was 8 years old, Haile Thomas, of New Windsor, New York, learned that her dad had type II diabetes. "We found out that food could be both the cause and the cure," she remembers. Diabetes affects the way your body uses glucose, a type of sugar.

Her family began to learn about food and nutrition. They changed their eating habits and got more exercise. About a year later, her dad was better and the whole family was healthier.

By age 12, Haile wanted to share what she'd learned with other kids across the country. She started The HAPPY Organization, which stands for Healthy Active Positive Purposeful Youth. Its Web site is www.thehappyorg.org.

Haile teaches cooking and nutrition classes about reading food labels, researching ingredients, controlling serving sizes, and not eating too much sugar. "I love to be super creative with cooking," she says.

In the first 4 years, she helped over 8,000 kids and got national attention. She also became the youngest certified integrative nutrition health coach in the country. "We want every kid to know how to make healthy choices," she adds.

The Homeless Helper

The summer before fifth grade, Liam Hannon decided to take part in a reading program instead of going to camp. The program required participants to complete challenges, and Liam selected community service. Seeing the homeless people near his apartment building in Cambridge, Massachusetts, gave Liam an idea: He could make lunches for people in need in his neighborhood.

Liam, along with his dad, decided that they would feed the homeless people for a week. They made 20 bag lunches—each with a peanut butter and jelly sandwich, piece of fruit, snack such as granola, and bottle of water. Liam also included notes in the lunches with sentiments like "Have a good day" or "Try to smile."

The people were surprised and happy to get the food. "When we give them the lunch and talk to them, they light up," Liam points out. At the end of the week, Liam and his dad wanted to help *more* people. They decided to make 60 lunches every week.

Liam's project is now known as Liam's Lunches of Love, and people have started donating food and money to help pay for the lunches. Every Sunday, the Hannons fill a wagon with lunches and walk through the neighborhood, giving them out. They are getting to know many of the people they feed. Liam says that the people "could just use a little kindness in their lives, and it feels really good to help."

The Science Whiz

Sixth-grader Gitanjali Rao loved learning about science and the environment. One day, her parents tested the household water in their Colorado home for unsafe chemicals. She learned that testing was expensive and did not always work (they had to do it several times) and wondered if there were a better way.

Gitanjali knew about the Discovery Education 3M Young Scientist Challenge, a competition for inventive kids. She had an idea for testing water, sent it in—and she became a finalist! This meant that she could work with a real scientist during the summer and together they could try to bring her idea to life.

To help, her parents set up a "science room" in their home, and Gitanjali used the labs of nearby schools. After 3 months of hard work, she had developed a device and app to test water for lead. She called it Tethys, after the Greek goddess of fresh water.

Gitanjali and the nine other finalists presented their projects to the judges, and she and Tethys got the highest score. She was named America's Top Young Scientist and won the grand prize of $25,000. "I was amazed!" Gitanjali says. She plans to continue to improve on her device, testing it for accuracy and making it more compact.

The Advice Writer

Everything changed for 8-year-old Shervin Azar when his family moved from Iran to Toronto, Ontario. He had to get used to a new country, culture, and language.

The first few months of school were tough. "I was really communicative in Iran, but here I was like a mouse," he recalls. Luckily, he had three Iranian classmates who translated for him. But even more changes followed. His dad's job forced the family to move to three different provinces in just 2 years. Finally, they settled in Abbotsford, British Columbia.

Shervin really wanted to share what he'd learned about moving to a new place with other kids, especially other young immigrants.

At age 11, he began to write a book. He published *Dare to Dream: Tweens' Road to Success* when he was 12. It had taken 3 months of research, 6 months of writing, and 3 months of rewriting. "When I first came to Canada almost 4 years ago," he wrote, "I thought that it would be impossible to learn a new language, impossible to fit into my new community, and impossible to be a Canadian. But here's the thing: Nothing is impossible! You can achieve anything you want if you just take tiny steps toward your goals. In fact, impossible is possible!"

After he mastered English, he began studying French, and he plans to write more books.

The Animal Rescuers

When 14-year-olds Hailey Amos (left) and Kylie Greene were Girl Scouts, they wanted to do a service project for their hometown, Bakersfield, California. They researched and discovered that about 40,000 pets a year die from smoke inhalation due to house fires. They learned about special pet oxygen masks that could save animals, including cats, dogs, and rabbits.

To raise money, Hailey and Kylie sold t-shirts and ice cream. They made $2,400 and bought masks for all 37 of the city's fire engines. "It was the perfect project for us," Kylie recalls, "because we got to help all animals—we love animals!—and we got to help the fire department." The good deed also earned the girls a Silver Award, one of Girl Scout's highest honors.

When a house caught fire in Bakersfield, the family pet, a shih tzu named Jack, went missing. Firefighter Matt Smith searched the home and finally located Jack. He carried him outside, laid him on the grass, and then covered his nose with a mask. After a minute or two, Jack began to breathe normally. Then he stood up, looking alert.

A month after the fire, Kylie and Hailey met Jack at Bakersfield Fire Station #1. Jack's owner said, "I really do thank them for their efforts to provide all these fire engines with this mask."

READY, SET, Success!

MEET FIVE **FASCINATING FOLKS** WHO MADE THEIR **MARK ON HISTORY.**

"Nellie Bly," Newspaper Reporter

When 16-year-old Elizabeth Jane Cochran saw an 1880 newspaper article about how a woman's place was in the home, she wrote a letter to the editor, disagreeing. The paper hired her as a reporter. Taking the name "Nellie Bly" to hide her identity, Elizabeth began a journalism career that eventually covered bad conditions in hospitals, adventuresome travel, battles of World War I, and women's fight for the right to vote. When she passed away at age 57, one paper called her "the Best Reporter in America."

Jordan Romero & Malavath Poorna, Everest Climbers

On May 21, 2010, Jordan Romero, of Big Bear Lake, California, became the youngest boy—at the age of 13 years, 10 months—to reach the top of the world's highest peak, Mt. Everest, on the border between Tibet (China) and Nepal. India's Malavath Poorna became the youngest girl—at 13 years, 11 months—to make the climb when she did it on May 25, 2014. Such youthful climbers sparked an ongoing debate about the safety of such climbs, and there are now some age restrictions.

William Kamkwamba, African Inventor

Growing up in Malawi, William Kamkwamba realized that a windmill could provide his village with much-needed electricity. When he was 14, he used ideas from books plus his own ingenuity to build one from bicycle and tractor parts, pieces of wood, junk from the local scrapyard, bottle caps, and even rubber from old flip-flops. Today, William continues to use his inventive creativity to help others in his beloved homeland.

Nick Young, Sharp-Eyed Sailor

As a cabin boy aboard the ship *Endeavour* on Captain James Cook's expedition to the South Seas in 1768–71, 12-year-old Nick Young served as a lookout in the crow's nest atop one of the ship's masts. On October 6, 1769, he was the first to sight a New Zealand bluff that Cook then named "Young Nick's Head" (a headland, or "head," is a high point of land above water). On July 10, 1771, he was the first to spot Land's End, England, on *Endeavour*'s return home.

WHERE DO WE GET OUR FOOD?

You probably know that ketchup is made from tomatoes that are grown on plants and that french fries are made from potatoes that grow underground. But what about some of the other foods you eat?

HUMMUS

Chickpeas (aka garbanzo beans) are the main ingredient in hummus. In the United States, the largest crops come from Washington and Idaho; in Canada, Alberta and Saskatchewan grow the most.

Chickpea plants need warm weather to grow. After the plants flower, they produce small, hairy pods with one to three chickpeas inside. They are ready to harvest when the plants wither and turn brown. The chickpeas will be tan or pale yellow and hard to the touch.

Hummus is made from crushed, cooked chickpeas. Other ingredients are added, such as garlic, sesame paste, lemon juice, or olive oil. Sometimes spices, peppers, or other vegetables are added for taste. Hummus is super-healthy for you and will boost your energy.

FOOD FACTS

■ The earliest mention of hummus appears in a cookbook from 13th-century Egypt.

■ *Hummus* is an Arabic word meaning chickpea.

■ The Guinness world record for the biggest plate of hummus was set in Beirut, Lebanon, in 2010 by a dish that weighed 23,042 pounds, 12 ounces!

TASTY HUMMUS

YOU WILL NEED:
blender or food
  processor
container with lid
1 can (15 ounces)
  chickpeas, drained
¼ cup olive oil
1 tablespoon lemon juice
1 teaspoon sesame oil

1. Put all of the ingredients into the blender and process until smooth.

2. Put hummus into container with lid and keep refrigerated.

3. Use hummus as a sandwich spread or a dip for vegetables, pita chips, or pretzels.

Convert to metric on p. 187

RICE

Rice is grown on every continent except Antarctica. In the United States, it is grown in the southern states and California. Rice starts as a seed and is planted in dry fields in the spring. Once planted, the fields are flooded with water. About 4 months after plants start growing, the fields are drained. The rice is ready for picking in late summer. Farmers use machines to cut the rice stalks and separate the rice kernels. The kernels are put into machines that constantly blow warm air to dry them. Once dried, the kernels are stored in silos or big bins. When the rice is ready to process, machines separate the kernels from the inedible hulls and remove any remaining debris. The kernels are still coated with a layer of bran. For brown rice, this layer is left alone. White rice is brown rice with the bran layer removed. The kernels are polished to be made brighter. White rice is then enriched with a coating of nutrients to replace those that were removed when the bran layer was stripped away.

FOOD FACTS

■ Rice is one of the oldest known foods that is still eaten today. Archaeologists have dated rice back to 7000 B.C.

■ Americans eat about 26 pounds of rice per person per year. Canadians eat about 15 pounds of rice per person per year.

■ Black, purple, and red rice varieties are grown in China and countries in South Asia.

GROW YOUR OWN RICE

YOU WILL NEED: water   large, deep bucket
½ cup organic long-   soil   ruler
  grain brown rice   compost   baking sheet with sides

1. Soak rice in water for 36 hours, then drain it.

2. Mix enough soil and compost to fill the bucket 6 inches deep.

3. Add water until it is about 2 inches above the soil surface.

4. Sprinkle rice on top of the water (it will sink), then place the bucket in a warm, sunny spot.

5. As the days pass, add water as needed to cover the soil.

6. After a few months, harvest your rice when the stalks turn yellow.

7. Cut the stalks and let them dry in a warm place for a couple of weeks.

8. Remove rice kernels by gently rubbing the tops of the stalks between your hands. Place kernels on baking sheet.

9. Preheat oven to 170°F. Put baking sheet in the oven for about 1 hour. Let kernels cool and remove hulls by pressing kernels hard between your fingers.

RAISINS

Raisins are dried grapes. Most raisin grapes in the United States are grown in California. The most popular raisin grape is 'Thompson Seedless'. Golden raisins (also called "sultanas") are usually dried muscat grapes. Some currants are also raisins, starting as 'Black Corinth' grapes.

Grapes grow on vines in vineyards. When the grapes are ripe, there are several ways to dry them: They can be cut off the vines by hand and laid out on trays in the sun to dry. They can also be placed in an oven or fruit dehydrator. Or they can be dried on the vine and harvested by machines. The raisins are stored in wooden bins until processing time, when they have their stems removed and are then sorted by size and washed.

MAKE YOUR OWN RAISINS

YOU WILL NEED:
small seedless grapes
baking sheet with sides
thin kitchen towel or
    cheesecloth

1. On a summer day, wash, dry, and de-stem the grapes.

2. Put grapes on the baking sheet in a single layer, making sure that they are not touching, then cover with the towel.

3. Put the baking sheet outdoors in full sun during the day and bring it back indoors at night. Repeat.

4. After a few days, depending on the weather, you now should have raisins!

FOOD FACTS

■ Raisins were once so valuable that Romans used them as money.

■ The word "raisin" comes from the Latin word *racemus*, which means a cluster of grapes or berries.

■ It takes 4 pounds of grapes to make 1 pound of raisins.

MUSTARD

Mustard plants are grown all over the world, but 85 percent of the ones that are used to make mustard are grown in Montana, North Dakota, and Canada. The plants produce yellow flowers and lots of small pods filled with seeds. When the pods turn brown, gardeners cut the stalks below the pods and put them into paper bags to finish drying. After a couple of weeks, the pods will split open and the seeds can be harvested.

The tiny seeds are crushed or ground into mustard powder. The powder can be used as a spice, or it can be added to water, vinegar, and other spices to make the kind of "prepared" mustard that you squirt on a hot dog.

White mustard seeds are used to make yellow mustard. A spice called turmeric is added to give mustard its bright yellow color. Brown and black seeds are used to make hotter mustards.

FOOD FACTS

◼ Ancient Greeks used mustard to treat toothaches.

◼ Pope John XII liked mustard so much that he created a job called "Grand Moutardier du Pape" or Mustard Maker to the Pope.

SIMPLE PREPARED MUSTARD

YOU WILL NEED:
bowl
wooden spoon
container with lid
5 tablespoons apple-cider vinegar
3 tablespoons water
½ cup ground mustard
1 teaspoon sugar or honey
¼ teaspoon salt

1. In the bowl, stir together vinegar and water.

2. Add ground mustard, sugar, and salt and stir until mixture is smooth.

3. Put mustard into container with lid and keep refrigerated.

POPCORN

Popcorn was first grown in what is now Mexico over 4,000 years ago. Today, more corn is grown and eaten in the United States than anywhere else in the world.

Corn grown for popcorn is different from the sweet corn that is grown for eating off the cob. One difference is easy to see: The silky brown tassels at the tip of a sweet corn husk stand straight up, but those on popcorn plants are floppy. When its tassels dry up and kernels are hard to the touch, popcorn is ready for picking. The cobs are dried for 8 to 12 months after harvest, then the kernels are cut from the cobs. The kernels are stored in bins with constant air circulation to dry them out even more. Once the kernels reach a 14 percent moisture level (the ideal level for popping), they are packaged for sale.

When heat is applied to the dried kernels, the moisture still trapped inside turns into steam, which bursts the outer shells and releases the soft, fluffy inner flakes of the kernels.

FOOD FACTS

■ Popcorn machines "popped up" in movie theaters in 1938.

■ A popped kernel can zoom up to 3 feet in the air!

■ Americans eat more than 13 billion quarts of popcorn each year, while Canadians eat about 1.6 billion quarts.

POPCORN GRANOLA MUNCH

YOU WILL NEED:
baking sheet with sides
nonstick cooking spray
large bowl
saucepan
rubber spatula
8 cups popped popcorn
 (about ½ cup of kernels)
1 cup wheat germ
1 cup old-fashioned oats
½ cup shredded coconut (optional)
½ cup peanuts or sesame seeds
½ cup creamy peanut or sunflower seed butter
½ cup molasses
2 tablespoons honey
1 tablespoon canola oil
1 tablespoon water

1. Preheat oven to 300°F.

2. Mist baking sheet with nonstick cooking spray.

3. In the bowl, combine popcorn, wheat germ, oats, coconut (if using), and peanuts.

4. In the saucepan over medium-low heat, combine peanut butter, molasses, honey, oil, and water. Stir with spatula while mixture cooks.

5. When completely melted, drizzle peanut butter mixture over popcorn mixture. Stir with spatula so the popcorn gets covered.

6. Spread mixture on baking sheet and bake for 30 minutes, stirring every 10 minutes.

In a Pickle

Whether you're sweet or sour on pickles, you'll relish this piece about preserving.

Pickles have been around for thousands of years. Greek philosopher Aristotle, Italian explorer Christopher Columbus, and English playwright William Shakespeare all ate pickles. Before refrigeration was available in homes, pickling was an important way to make food safe for storing at home and on long journeys. Pickling produce provided families with food throughout the cold winter months. Pickles can be sweet, sour, salty, or hot or any combination of these. Although cucumbers are believed to be the first vegetables that were pickled, virtually any fruit or vegetable will do. Asparagus? Yes! Watermelon? Yes! Pumpkin? Yes!

The Pickling Process

Pickles are made by covering fresh vegetables and fruit with vinegar or a saltwater brine. The vinegar and brine keep the pickles crisp and prevent the growth of bacteria. Flavorings such as mustard seeds, coriander seeds, peppercorns, cinnamon, dill, ginger, and garlic are often added.

A Peck of Pickled Plums

Around the world, nearly every country and cuisine has its own favorite pickle based on what is local and available. In Japan, cooks pickle plums and call them *umeboshi*. *Giardiniera,* a combination of pickled peppers, celery, cauliflower, and carrots, is an Italian specialty. In Morocco, folks enjoy *l'hamd markad,* or pickled lemons.

Pickle Power

■ To store pickles safely for several months, they must be processed in a boiling-water bath. Check with an adult before you attempt this method.

■ The word "pickle" comes from the Dutch word *pekel* or Old German *pökel*, meaning "salt" or "brine."

■ To be "in a pickle" means to be in a difficult situation.

■ Have you ever played pickleball? Invented in 1965, this sport is a combination of tennis, badminton, and Ping-Pong.

■ Try this tongue twister first published in 1813:
Peter Piper picked a peck of pickled peppers;
A peck of pickled peppers Peter Piper picked.
If Peter Piper picked a peck of pickled peppers,
Where's the peck of pickled peppers Peter Piper picked?

■ Cleopatra claimed that eating pickles helped to keep her healthy and beautiful.

■ During an excruciatingly hot (109°F!) football game on September 3, 2000, the Philadelphia Eagles beat the Dallas Cowboys 41–14. The Eagles credited their win to drinking pickle juice during the game to prevent dehydration and muscle cramps.

■ In some homes on Christmas Eve, it is tradition to hide a pickle ornament in the branches of the Christmas tree. The first child to spot the pickle on Christmas morning is said to be destined for good luck in the coming year—and also has the privilege of opening the first present.

■ Use the brine left over from a jar of store-bought pickles to marinate vegetables overnight. Pour it on sliced zucchini, baby carrots, or trimmed green beans.

You can easily make your own pickles. For the following recipe, use fresh cucumbers from a local farmers' market, farm stand, or your own garden. Do not use the waxy kind found at the supermarket. The wax coating prevents the vinegar or brine from penetrating the pickles.

Sweet Refrigerator Pickles

YOU WILL NEED:
colander or strainer
2 bowls
large container with a lid
6 to 8 medium cucumbers, sliced
2 onions, sliced
2 red bell peppers, sliced
3 hot peppers, sliced
1 tablespoon pickling salt
2 cups sugar
2 cups apple cider vinegar
2 teaspoons celery seed
2 teaspoons mustard seed

Convert to metric on p. 187

1. Place the colander over one of the bowls. Add the cucumbers, onions, and peppers. Sprinkle with the salt and set aside for 1 hour. Drain the liquid that collects in the bowl.

2. In a separate bowl, stir together sugar, vinegar, celery seeds, and mustard seeds until the sugar is dissolved. Pour vegetables into the bowl and stir. Transfer to a large glass or plastic container with a cover and store in the refrigerator.

3. These pickles can be eaten right away, but the flavor is better after about 1 week. They will keep for 1 month in the refrigerator.

Makes about 4 quarts.

DairyGood Recipes

Do you like yogurt, butter, and ricotta cheese? With a few simple ingredients, you can make them yourself!

Yum!
Top your homemade yogurt with fruit or granola. If you want to sweeten it, stir a little bit of honey or maple syrup into individual servings.

Yay for Yogurt!

YOU WILL NEED:
large pot with a lid
food-grade thermometer
wooden spoon
ladle
bowl
whisk
kitchen towels
container with lid
1 quart whole milk
¼ cup plain yogurt containing active cultures

1. Pour the milk into the large pot and put on the stove over medium heat. Hold the thermometer in the milk and heat to 200°F, stirring gently to keep the milk from burning or boiling.

Convert to metric on p. 187

2. Remove the pot from the heat and let the milk cool to 115°F. Stir occasionally to prevent a skin from forming on top.

3. Using the ladle, scoop a cup of the warm milk into the bowl and add the yogurt. Whisk until the yogurt is completely mixed with the milk. Pour it into the pot of milk, whisking slowly.

4. Cover the pot with its lid, wrap it in a couple of towels, and place it in the oven, but do not turn the oven on. Close the oven door.

5. After 4 hours, taste test the yogurt. Do this every 15 minutes until it has a flavor and consistency that you like. Remove the pot from the oven and whisk the yogurt once more.

6. Transfer the yogurt to a container with a lid and refrigerate. It will stay fresh for about 2 weeks.

Makes about 4 cups.

Yum! Spread your homemade butter on biscuits or bagels or melt some on top of noodles.

Better Butter

YOU WILL NEED:
1 quart glass jar with lid
container with lid
2 cups heavy cream

1. Pour the cream into the jar and screw the lid on tight.

2. Shake the jar up and down and side to side, but keep a firm hold on it. Take turns shaking the jar with a sibling or friend. The cream will begin to thicken and stop sloshing around—at this point, you will have whipped cream!

3. Keep shaking, and after a few more minutes you will hear liquid sloshing around again as the buttermilk separates from the butter that's forming inside the jar. Shake the jar for a few minutes longer, until the butter is a solid ball.

4. Open the jar and drain off the buttermilk. Remove the butter and clean it by rinsing under cold water. Rinsing removes any remaining buttermilk and will help to keep the butter fresh.

5. Transfer the butter to a container with a lid and refrigerate. It will stay fresh for about 2 weeks.

Makes about ½ cup.

Ricotta Cheese, Please!

YOU WILL NEED:

large pot	cheesecloth	½ gallon whole milk
food-grade thermometer	strainer	⅓ cup lemon juice, plus more as needed
wooden spoon	bowl	
	slotted spoon	
	container with lid	½ teaspoon salt

1. Pour the milk into the large pot and put on the stove over medium heat. Hold the thermometer in the milk and heat to 200°F, stirring gently to keep the milk from burning or boiling.

2. Remove the milk from the heat and add the lemon juice and salt. Stir to combine. Let the milk sit for 10 minutes.

3. Check the milk to see if it has separated into small clumps of white curds and yellow, watery whey. If the curds and whey haven't separated yet, add another tablespoon of lemon juice, stir, and wait for a few more minutes before checking again.

4. Place the cheesecloth in the strainer, covering the holes. Set the strainer over the bowl. Using the slotted spoon, scoop the curds from the pot and put them into the strainer. Slowly pour the remaining curds and whey through the strainer. Let the curds drain for 20 minutes to 1 hour, depending on how wet you like your ricotta cheese (and how impatient you are to try it!). Discard liquid.

5. Transfer the ricotta to a container with a lid and refrigerate. It will stay fresh for up to a week.

Makes about 2 cups.

> **Yum!**
> Try your homemade ricotta on pizza or spread some on toast and top with sliced bananas, chopped walnuts, and a drizzle of honey.

LET THE GAMES BEGIN!

Enjoy these four simple outdoor games that don't require any fancy equipment.

In Your Toes

How prehensile* are your toes?

YOU WILL NEED:
1 hula hoop
a bunch of marbles
as many players as you like

Get Ready . . .
Put the hula hoop on a flat surface (grass, floor, sidewalk).

Get Set . . .
Scatter the marbles inside the hoop.

Go!
Standing with one foot outside the hoop, each person in turn tries to pick up as many marbles as possible, one at a time, with their other foot and transfer them outside the hoop. The person who gets the most marbles out in 1 minute is the winner.

DID YOU KNOW?
*"Prehensile" means adapted for seizing or grasping. Some New World primates, such as howler monkeys, woolly monkeys, and spider monkeys, have prehensile tails that can grab a tree branch or vine and hold the monkey's weight so that the animal can swing through the trees.

S
P
O
R
T
S

Beanbag Tic-Tac-Toe

This is an outdoor version of the classic game.

YOU WILL NEED:
4 long, straight sticks (yardsticks work well if you can't find sticks)
10 beanbags (5 each in two different colors) or 10 small zipper-
close bags (5 each filled with a different type of dried beans)
2 players

Get Ready . . .
Lay out the sticks on the ground in the familiar tic-tac-toe formation.

Get Set . . .
Mark a spot where the tossers stand (this can be adjusted to the age
and skills of the tosser). Choose your beanbag color.

Go!
The players take turns tossing a beanbag. The goal is to get three
bags in a straight line—up, down, or diagonal across the grid, just as
in the tic-tac-toe game that you play on paper.

DID YOU KNOW?
In 1952, English computer scientist Sandy Douglas wrote
a program that he called "Noughts and Crosses" (the
English name for tic-tac-toe) on an early computer called
EDSAC. The program's name was later changed to OXO.

Drip, Drip, Drop

Here's a watery version of Duck, Duck, Goose for hot summer days (bathing suits recommended!).

YOU WILL NEED:
1 small plastic cup
clean water
as many players as you like

Get Ready . . .
All but one of the players sit in a circle.

Get Set . . .
One person is "It." He or she fills the plastic cup with water.

Go!
"It" walks around the circle, dripping water on each player's head in passing and saying "Drip" each time. When "It" says "Drop!," however, he or she dumps the cupful of water on a sitting player's head and then runs around the circle in the same direction, chased by the person who got wet. If "It" can get back to the target person's spot before being tagged, the target person becomes "It" and the game starts again. If tagged before getting there, he or she stays "It" for another round.

DID YOU KNOW?
In Minnesota, children play the game of Duck, Duck, Gray Duck instead of Duck, Duck, Goose. No one knows for sure the reason why this name is used only in Minnesota, but it may be because Duck, Duck, Gray Duck originated in Sweden and many Minnesotans are of Swedish descent.

Nine Pins

This is just like bowling, but you don't have to wear special shoes!

YOU WILL NEED:
9 empty 1-liter plastic bottles
a ball that's smaller than the bottles
as many players as you like

Get Ready . . .
Set up the bottles in a diamond formation (1-2-3-2-1) on a smooth, flat surface, with one point facing the bowler.

Get Set . . .
Have the bowler back up to an agreed distance (which can be adjusted for younger bowlers).

Go!
Roll or toss the ball at the bottles, trying to knock down as many as you can! The one who knocks down the most bottles wins. Reset the bottles for another round after each bowler's turn. Add up how many bottles each person has knocked over. Stop after 10 rounds and add up every bowler's score.

DID YOU KNOW?
Bowling is one of our oldest games. Sir Flinders Petrie, a British archeologist, found objects in a child's grave in Egypt that appeared to have been used in a game similar to bowling. The items were more than 5,000 years old!

CURLERS

ARE COOL!

Folks have been playing the sport of curling since the 16th century. Today, it is gaining popularity in both the United States and Canada.

Curling originated in Scotland, where it was played on frozen ponds and lakes. The Scottish word *curr* means a low rumble, and this is how the game got its name: A curling stone makes a low rumble as it slides on ice. Sometimes the rumble can be loud, which is why the sport was once nicknamed "the roaring game."

A STONE, A BROOM, AND SHOES

Curling stones, also called rocks, are made of a special type of granite found at either Ailsa Craig, a small island off the coast of Scotland, or the Trefor Granite Quarry in Wales. Each one is polished and shaped to be 36 inches around and at least 4½ inches tall and to weigh between 38 and 44 pounds. Handles attached to the top enable players to grip and rotate (spin) a stone when playing.

Convert to metric on p. 187

Brooms made with bristles of hog hair, horsehair, or synthetic fabric are used by players to sweep the ice in front of a moving stone. Sweeping takes skill: Sweeping quickly clears away debris and melts

a thin layer of ice, which makes the stone go fast and straight; slower sweeping will slow down a stone and cause it to curl. Sweepers take direction from the Skip, whose advice enables them to stop the stone in exactly the right place.

Curling shoes are specially made for playing on ice. The sole of one shoe is covered with rubber that grips the ice so that a player will not easily fall down; the other sole is smooth, enabling a player to glide.

IT'S BETTER WITH BUMPS

The earliest curlers played outdoors on frozen ponds where, naturally, the ice was rough or bumpy due to pebbles, twigs, and the weather. Today, tiny bumps are made on the ice, even at indoor rinks, so that the game can be played under authentic conditions. Two layers of water droplets are sprinkled on the ice and each layer is allowed to freeze. Curlers call this "pebbling." The bumps reduce friction, enabling the stones to move faster.

HOW TO PLAY

The game consists of 10 "ends" (think of innings or periods in other sports). Each team has four players who take turns sliding stones forward on the "curling sheet"—a long (150 feet!), narrow strip of ice—toward a target area called the "house." The target contains three colored rings, usually red, white, and blue. The smallest and innermost ring is the "button" or "tee."

While a player's stone is moving down the ice, team members sweep near it to control its speed and direction.

Each team throws eight stones; after 16 stones are played, the one closest to the tee within or touching the house wins the end. This stone's team gets a point for each stone closer to the tee than their opponent's nearest stone. The opposing team scores no points for this end.

After 10 ends (or more, if the score is tied), the team with the most total points wins the game.

MEET THE TEAM

Each team has four members:

The Lead throws the first and second stones and then sweeps for the next six stones.

The Second throws the third and fourth stones and then sweeps for the other six stones.

The Third throws the fifth and sixth stones and sweeps for the first four stones.

The Skip is the captain. He or she throws the seventh and eighth stones, calls directions to sweepers, and decides the team's strategy for winning the end.

THE SPIRIT OF CURLING

Good sportsmanship and etiquette are important in curling. Games start and end with handshakes between the teams, and players congratulate their opponents when they make a good shot. After each game, players shake hands with their opponents, saying, "Good curling."

CURLING FOR GOLD

Men's curling was part of the first Olympic Games in 1924, where Great Britain defeated Sweden and France. Curling did not appear in the Olympics as a medal sport again until 1998.

The U.S. Curling team won its first gold medal in 2018; Canada has won six gold medals in the sport.

STONE COLD

Before a curling stone is used for play, it is cooled to be the same temperature as the ice. Players put stones into walk-in freezers or home-made wooden boxes that sit on the ice. Cooling prevents damage to the stones.

Fishing for Fun

Human beings have invented many ways to catch fish, but the simplest is to attach a line with a hook on the end of it to a pole and drop the hook into the water. Throwing the line is called *casting*. A good angler (another name for someone who fishes, because the hook is a piece of metal that is bent at an *angle*) can cast the hook into a small patch of water right where the fish are hanging out.

It takes time to get good at casting. Here's a fun way to practice casting into the right spot, like an expert angler. All you need is a fishing pole, a line with a *bobber* (a little plastic ball that floats on the water and shows when a fish has taken the bait by *bobbing* up and down), and a hula hoop for a target. If you don't have a hula hoop, you could use some string or rope shaped into a circle. There is no need for a hook on your line at this point.

Find a patch of grass or dirt where there are no bushes or tree branches to snag your line. Place the target on the ground about 10 feet away and try to cast your bobber into the hoop. Cast from your side rather than over your head. You're less likely to get the line tangled in your clothes or around your fishing buddy.

It will take some patience and persistence before you get it into the hoop. Once you can do that, move the hoop farther away, until you can cast your bobber 20 or even 30 feet and land it inside the target.

Invite friends to try it with you, and see who can put the bobber in the hoop most often and from the greatest distance away. Soon, you will be ready to go to a stream or pond and look for a quiet patch of water where fish might be lurking. But don't forget a hook with some bait or a lure!

Fishy Facts

■ Fishing is one of the oldest human activities on Earth. People were carving fish hooks from seashells 23,000 years ago.

■ John Dennys, who wrote *The Secrets of Angling* in 1613, was said to have fished with William Shakespeare.

■ A person who studies fish is called an ichthyologist.

■ The moonfish is the only warm-blooded fish discovered so far.

■ Some fish "talk" to each other by contracting their flotation bladder, which creates vibrations.

Fish Tale

A young man named William Wainwright was fishing near Exeter, New Hampshire, in March 1860, when he offered a stranger his extra pole. The two fished until dark but never exchanged their names. Later, William discovered that his fellow angler was Abraham Lincoln, who was visiting his son, Robert, a student at Phillips Exeter Academy. One year later, Abraham Lincoln would be sworn in as president.

How the Became a

In China, the pig symbolized wealth and abundance. On farms, the pig served as a way to grow wealth. Farmers fed their pig leftover food until it was large enough to sell for meat. A very large pig meant that the family could sell some meat for money and keep some for food. The pig was a poor person's moneybox: Its value increased with its size.

Based on this, long ago, some people who hoped to become wealthy by saving cash began making pig-shape containers for storing their coins. They fed their pig banks leftover money—what we might call spare change—until they were full. The oldest pig bank around today was found in Indonesia and is at least 500 years old. But these banks were used long before that.

Banks in the shape of a pig first appeared in Europe around the 1400s. Most of these banks were made of ceramic or porcelain (and later, cast iron). Early piggy banks had a slot for putting coins into the body but no hole for removing them. To get the money out, a bank had to be broken. As a result, there are few old banks in existence. (Today, most piggy banks have a hole with a plug in the belly for removing money.)

PIG BANK

Pig tales from different cultures help to uncover the history and mystery.

Pygg, Pug, Pig

An English legend involves orange clay used for making dishes, bowls, pots, and washbasins. The word for the clay was pygg, pronounced "pug." For centuries, Europeans saved their money in orange clay pots—pygg pots—in their homes, because there was no banking system. Over the years, the pronunciation of pygg evolved into "pig."

This Little Piggy

- In the Netherlands and Germany, a piggy bank is often given as a gift for a newborn baby. The bank, which represents good luck and prosperity, is filled with money to begin building the child's fortune.

- In Germany, piggy banks are given as New Year gifts to bring good luck.

- In the United States, piggy banks are given to children to encourage them to save money.

- The Jewish and Muslim religions consider the pig an unclean animal, so followers do not own or eat pigs. Not many piggy banks will be found in Jewish or Muslim homes.

Did You Know?

- A large bronze piggy bank named Rachel at Pike Place Market in Seattle serves as a mascot for The Market Foundation. She weighs

550 pounds and has collected over $350,000 since 1986.

- The world's largest piggy bank, created by a German savings bank in May 2015, was 18 feet 3.7 inches tall and 26 feet 4.3 inches long. It was painted red.

Make a Papier-Mâché Piggy

YOU WILL NEED:

1 balloon	newspaper	2 cups water
1 paper towel roll	bowl	paint and
tape	1 cup all-purpose	paintbrushes
cardboard	flour	stickers (optional)

1. The balloon is your mold. Blow it up to your desired piggy bank size.

2. Cut the paper towel roll into five pieces to serve as the feet and snout. Tape the feet and snout to the balloon.

3. Cut ears out of the cardboard. Tape them to your piggy bank's head.

4. Tear newspaper into strips 1 to 2 inches wide and in a variety of lengths.

5. In the bowl, combine the flour and water. Stir to make a smooth paste.

6. Dip one strip of newspaper into the paste, coating it thoroughly. Hold the strip between two fingers of one hand and, with the other hand, pull it through your fingers to remove the excess paste.

7. Lay the strip on the mold. Gently smooth in place. Repeat, overlapping the strips and laying them in different directions. When the balloon is covered, and each time you add layers, set it aside to dry thoroughly and put a cover on the paste. Repeat the process until you are satisfied. (We recommend at least four layers.)

8. When completely dry, cut a slot in the top of the pig. This will pop the balloon. Remove the balloon through the slot. Paint or decorate your piggy bank.

REVOLUTIONARY MINUTES

TWO GENERALS AND A DOG

General George Washington and the Continental Army lost the Battle of Germantown, Pennsylvania, on October 4, 1777. Sir William Howe, leader of the British troops, won the battle but lost his dog.

Perhaps frightened by gun blasts and the chaos of conflict on that foggy day, the dog wandered off. Two days later, it appeared in the Americans' camp, where it came to the attention of General Washington.

The commander checked the dog's tag and saw that it belonged to General Howe! Washington ordered the dog fed and groomed and then had a message sent to his enemy:

General Washington's compliments to General Howe. He does himself the pleasure to return him a Dog, which accidentally fell into his hands, and by the inscription on the Collar appears to belong to General Howe.

The dog's name is not known, nor is there any official record of General Howe's response. Washington's note survives alone.

DID YOU KNOW? General Washington had his aide Alexander Hamilton write the note to General Howe. A draft of the note is kept at the Library of Congress.

MIDNIGHT RIDER MISCONCEPTIONS

Paul Revere did not ride his own horse through the suburbs of Boston, Massachusetts, on April 18, 1775, to warn the local people that British soldiers were about to march from that city into the countryside. He did not own a horse, and the first stage of his journey that night was by boat: He was rowed across the Charles River to Charlestown, Massachusetts, a town north of Boston.

For the stage of the journey on land, Revere borrowed "a very good horse" from John Larkin, a local merchant. The name of the horse is not known; people seldom gave horses names in those days. Revere did not shout "The British are coming!" during his ride because many colonists were British and he had to avoid British patrols to carry out his secret mission.

DID YOU KNOW? Since 1914, the National Lancers have reenacted Paul Revere's ride on horseback every year on Patriots Day. Large crowds gather to watch them pass by.

HEROINE ON HORSEBACK

On April 25, 1777, British soldiers marched into Danbury, Connecticut, and almost immediately set fire to the storehouses that held sugar, molasses, coffee, corn, flour, and wheat, as well as clothing and hospital cots and tents belonging to the Continental Army. Word of the attack reached the home of Colonel Henry Ludington, commander of the militia in Kent, New York, at 9:00 P.M. The messenger, who was unfamiliar with the area, arrived exhausted from the journey and soaked by rain.

Only one person there besides the colonel knew the countryside well enough to alert the militia: his daughter, 16-year-old Sybil, the oldest of the 12 Ludington children. While the colonel made preparations for his men, Sybil set out, shouting the news that roused the militia to arms. She rode until dawn, covering 40 miles while avoiding British soldiers and loyalists, as well as outlaws. Colonel Ludington and his men arrived too late to save Danbury, but they fought the British as they departed.

DID YOU KNOW? Today, Sybil Ludington is known as the female Paul Revere.

The eye is
the jewel of
the body.

-Henry David Thoreau,
American writer
(1817–62)

The EYES Have It!

Your eyes are complex little body parts that allow you to see your best friend, look at a book, and watch a game of soccer. Each of your eyes is about the size of a Ping-Pong ball. Eyes have eyelids, lashes, and brows to help keep them safe and functioning properly. Eyelids open and close in order to spread fluid that keeps your eyes moist. Eyelashes and eyebrows keep dirt, debris, and sweat from getting into your eyes. These delicate organs require 24-hour protection!

Eye Exam

Your eye is made up of several parts:

☐ The white part of your eye is called the **sclera.** It is a tough, protective coating that covers most of the eyeball.

☐ The **iris** is the part of your eye that is colored. It contains muscles that adjust the size of the pupil. This controls the amount of light that enters the eye.

☐ The black circle in the center of the iris is called the **pupil.** In bright light, it shrinks to allow less light in; in low light, it widens.

☐ The clear tissue that covers the iris is called the **cornea.** It focuses the eye.

☐ The **lens** sits behind the iris and is clear. It projects light to the retina.

☐ The **retina**, at the back of the eye, is made up of millions of tiny rods and cones (so named because those are what they look like). The rods and cones capture light and allow you to see shapes and colors.

☐ The **optic nerve** carries the information gathered by the retina to your brain, where images are identified.

☐ The **vitreous humor** is the clear, jellylike material that fills the inside of the eye from the lens to the retina.

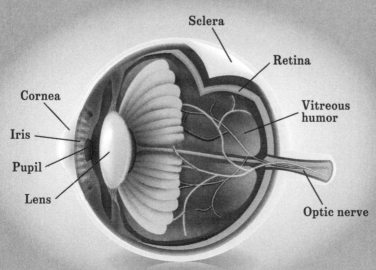

Sclera

Retina

Vitreous humor

Cornea

Iris

Pupil

Lens

Optic nerve

Wrong Way

Did you know that your eyes actually see everything upside down? Because the front part of the eye is curved, it bends light, which reflects an upside-down image to the retina. The optic nerve sends what it sees to the visual processing part of the brain, which flips the picture so that you see it the right way.

Pink Is a Problem

Pink eye, also known as conjunctivitis, often happens when an allergen, bacteria, or virus gets into your eye. An infected eye will look swollen and reddish pink, be itchy, and sometimes leak pus. Pink eye can spread very easily, so if you or someone you know has it, keep your hands to yourself and wash them often.

Roman Rule

Have you ever heard the phrase, "It's all fun and games until someone loses an eye"? It comes from ancient Rome, where wrestling matches had only one rule—no eye-gouging. If a wrestler hurt an opponent's eye or eyes, he was disqualified and the match ended.

Sleep Tight—Don't Let the Eye Boogers Bite

What is that yellow, crusty stuff sometimes in the corners of your eyes when you wake up in the morning? Although it goes by many names—sleep seeds, eye boogers, eye sand—it is mucus. The fluid that covers your eyes is made up of fatty oils (called "lipids"), water, salt, and mucus. As you sleep, the fluid keeps flowing. Your eyes might be closed, but they are not sealed shut, so some of the mucus seeps out and dries up.

Eye Didn't Know That!

- ☐ More people have brown eyes than those of any other color.
- ☐ *Heterochromia iridis* is the condition of having irises of two different colors.
- ☐ It is possible for eyes to get sunburned—protect them when you are outside!
- ☐ The fear of eyes is called *ommatophobia*.
- ☐ You shed one to five eyelashes every day.
- ☐ Each eye has about 120 million rods and 7 million cones.
- ☐ You blink about 15 to 20 times every minute.
- ☐ You blink more rapidly when you hear or see something unpleasant or are nervous.

THINGS TO KNOW ABOUT HAVING TO GO

Whether you call it "peeing," "answering the call of nature," or "making a pit stop," it's a natural function and everyone does it.

When you head to the bathroom to relieve yourself, you are doing your body a favor. Urine is about 95 percent water, but it also includes dead blood cells, sugar, salts, ammonia, hormones, and numerous chemicals that your body needs to get rid of.

Making Your Bladder Gladder

You may think that your bladder is the only organ responsible for urine, but your kidneys get in on the action, too. Kidneys have several functions, one of which is to remove the body's liquid waste matter. As blood flows through your kidneys, water and waste are filtered out. The wastewater gets sent on to your bladder, while the blood gets sent back through your bloodstream to your heart. Your bladder expands (think of a water balloon), and as it gets full, nerve endings in the bladder wall make you feel the urge to pee. This entire process creates about 1 to 2 quarts of urine every day.

Normal or Not?

If you drink enough water and are in good health, your urine should be pale yellow with a mild smell. If you haven't had enough water, it will be darker yellow and smell stronger, signaling you to drink up! When you eat a lot of beets or carrots or take certain vitamins, your urine could change to be slightly pink or orange in color. Some people will notice that their urine has a strong smell if they have recently eaten asparagus, onions, or garlic—this is normal. However, if you have the urge to go frequently, have a burning sensation, or have urine that is cloudy, foamy, brown, blue, green, or red or smells fishy, this could be a sign of an infection and you should see a doctor.

Gee, Whiz

For the past 2,000 years, people have been trying to figure out ways to utilize this free fluid. Some ancient Romans used urine to whiten their teeth. (We'll stick to toothpaste, thank you very much.) They also placed buckets along the streets so that people could pee into them. When the containers were full, the urine was used to wash dirty clothes at laundries because it proved to be good at removing stains.

Don't Try This at Home!

In the 1980s, automotive engineers needed harder metal in their engine blocks to stand up to the rigors of high speeds. After putting the engine blocks out in the cold, they peed on them, which hardened the metal.

Major league baseball player Moises Alou didn't wear batting gloves; he peed on his hands, saying that this toughened his skin.

Streaming History

In England during the 1500s, urine was used to brighten colors when dyeing cloth, which helped to make the country's fabrics famous. Early Europeans used urine instead of soap to clean their homes. (Ammonia, found in urine, is an important ingredient

in today's household cleaning products.) Later, people found that urine worked well at getting rid of hair and unwanted flesh from animal hides, so they used it to clean and soften leather. Urine was believed to be sterile (scientists still debate this), so if clean water wasn't available, urine was used in war zones to wash battle wounds before sewing them up.

Space Waste

On the International Space Station, astronauts pee into a special bag. After it passes through a filter and a sugar solution, the urine is turned into drinkable water. Similarly, people who have been lost at sea or stranded in a desert with no drinking water have drunk their urine to quench their thirst.

Sensible Solutions

Urine mixed with compost makes a great fertilizer. Scientists in Nepal found that they could grow taller plants with bigger harvests when they added urine to compost. In Nigeria, where electricity is scarce, a group of teenage girls invented an electrical generator that uses urine for fuel. This generator produces 6 hours of electricity on 1 liter of urine.

Convert to metric on p. 187

Go With the Flow

- Although people claim that urine is good for healing jellyfish stings, doctors don't believe that this works.
- On average, a person pees seven times a day.
- A human bladder can hold about 12 ounces of urine.
- The scientific name for peeing is micturition.
- A 7-year study conducted at the University of Alberta concluded that urine consists of over 3,000 different chemical compounds!

Cat Trick
SECRETS

With a few simple instructions, you can become a superstar cat trainer! This is a great way to bond and have fun with your pet. Plus, your cat will get some important mental and physical exercise, and the tricks will impress your family and friends.

Training 101

We all like to be appreciated for good behavior; your cat will want to be rewarded for performing tricks. Find something that she loves, such as a sliver of tuna or a bit of chicken. Next, find a marker—no, not the kind used for coloring. A "marker" is a word or a sound that "marks" the moment that an animal does what you have asked. When training dogs, a clicker is often used as a marker. Choose a word like "yes," click your tongue, or use a dog clicker for your marker. Every time that you use the marker, immediately reward your cat with the treat. It won't take her long to understand that the mark means that something good is coming her way.

Sitting Pretty

Hold a treat to her nose, then lift it up and move it just over her head. As she follows the treat, she will drop her bottom into a sit. Use your marker and give her the treat.

Once she is sitting for the treat every time, switch to luring her with an empty hand but still use your marker and give her a treat when her bottom touches the ground. Now you've taught a hand signal. You can add the word "Sit" once she has learned the trick and is giving you a sit for the hand signal.

Shake a Paw

Place a treat in your hand and let your cat smell it. Then close your hand into a fist and hold it in front of her. If she is interested, she will paw at your fist to get the treat. As soon as her paw touches your hand, use your marker and give her the treat. Once she is regularly touching your treat-filled fist, switch to an empty fist and, finally, to an open palm. As you go through these steps, remember to use your marker and give a treat every time that she gets it right. When she learns to touch your palm, add the cue "Shake a paw."

Come When Called

Before beginning, choose the words that you'll use to call your cat, such as "Here, Kitty, Kitty." It's best not to include her name, as to do so might be confusing when she hears her name at nontraining times.

Start by calling her when she is only a few feet away. Say "Here, Kitty, Kitty" and then shake a treat bag, dangle a toy, or do anything else that you can to catch her interest. When she starts to come toward you, use your marker and give her a treat.

As she learns that the cue "Here, Kitty, Kitty" means that a treat is on the way, she will be more likely to come when called. When she catches on, work your way up to calling her from another room.

I had been told that the training procedure with cats was difficult. It's not. Mine had me trained in two days.

–Bill Dana, American comedian (1924–2017)

Keep your attitude positive and your training sessions short. To your cat, this is just a game, so four or five tries is enough at one time. Once your cat has mastered her tricks, you don't have to use your marker anymore or give her treats every time. But to keep her interested in performing with you, be sure to treat her often. Even though you're the trainer, let her think that she is in charge and you can both have fun showing off all of her new tricks.

Pet-iculars

Dogs and cats are the most common pets,
but they often have plenty of company.
Find out how to care for your specialty pet
with some frequently asked questions.

Hamster Haven

Q: Should I put a water bottle or bowl in my hamster's home?

A: Hamsters love to drink water, and a bottle is best. Bottles are less likely to spill and make a wet mess. This is good for both you and your hamster: Wet messes mean constantly cleaning out the cage because hamsters prefer clean, dry bedding.

Q: Can I give my hamster a bath?

A: You should not bathe your hamster. A hamster's fur contains oils that help to keep it healthy, and giving it a bath would remove them. Hamsters are good at grooming and keeping themselves clean, but if you do notice a strong odor, it may mean that there is a problem and your hamster should see a veterinarian.

Q: Why does my hamster sleep so much during the day?

A: Hamsters are nocturnal, which means that they are active at night. This is a good reason not to keep a hamster cage in your bedroom. Your hamster will likely be working out on its wheel while you are trying to sleep, and this can be noisy.

Rabbit Roundup

Q: What vegetables can I feed my rabbit besides carrots?

A: Rabbits enjoy a variety of veggies like celery, bell peppers, broccoli leaves, leaf lettuce, and spinach. Treat your rabbit with fruit from time to time—try berries and peeled bananas and kiwi. If you are giving your rabbit a food that it has not eaten before, start with a small amount.

Q: Will my rabbit shed?

A: Rabbits shed their fur about four times a year. While rabbits do lick their fur to groom themselves, it is important that they do not ingest too much of it. Like cats, they get fur balls; unlike cats, they can not cough them up—instead, fur balls can cause digestive problems. Be sure to brush your rabbit at least once a week to help to remove shedding hair.

Q: Is it normal that my rabbit chews everything?

A: Rabbits do chew a lot, and this is a normal habit. Rabbits enjoy chewing, plus it is good for their teeth. Provide your rabbit with safe things to chew like a cotton towel, a basket filled with fresh hay (let them chew both!), and untreated pinecones.

Chinchilla Checklist

Q: How do I keep my chinchilla's coat soft and shiny?
A: Your chinchilla needs to take a dust bath several times a week to keep its coat beautiful. The bath eliminates excess moisture and oil from its coat. Dust created specifically for this purpose is available at most pet stores. Put a deep bowl filled with dust for your chinchilla's baths in its home. The bowl should be slightly larger than your chinchilla to allow it room to roll around. Remove the bowl when bath time is over.

Q: Why does my chinchilla eat its poop?
A: It may sound gross to us humans, but many animals—including chinchillas—eat their poop. The word for this habit is "coprophagy" (ka-PRAH-fa-jee). Chinchillas produce two kinds of poop—pellets, for removing waste, and cecotropes, for consuming. Cecotropes are full of nutrients that could not be digested the first time around and beneficial bacteria that keep your chinchilla healthy.

Q: How big will my chinchilla get?
A: Chinchillas usually grow to be between 9 and 15 inches long (the tail can add 3 to 6 inches). The average size is about 10 inches. An adult chinchilla will weigh between 1 and 2 pounds.

The HOWS of the DOWSE

Have you ever seen someone using a metal detector at a beach or park to search for buried "treasures"? Some folks "dowse," or use a forked stick to search for water or other items.

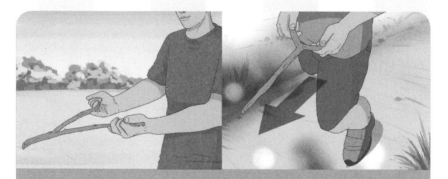

Dowsing is an ancient technique for finding underground items by using a handheld instrument. The most common use is to find water. No one knows for sure why dowsing works (or *if* it works!).

A person who practices dowsing is called a "dowser." The tools used by a dowser vary, but the traditional instrument is a Y-shape tree branch. Sometimes dowsers use a stick, a pair of L-shape metal rods, or a pendulum, which is simply a weight hung from a chain or string.

To find water, a dowser clears the mind and concentrates, trying to tune in to the energy of the underground water. The dowser walks back and forth over the area, alert to any movement of the dowsing tool. The stem end of the branch is expected to dip slightly toward the ground or twitch when a discovery is made.

The Proof Is in the Pulling

Dowsers claim that the only way to really understand dowsing is to experience it for yourself. So, give it a try!

1. With the help of an adult, find or cut a Y-shape branch from a tree. Branches from willows, fruit trees, and witch hazel are considered excellent dowsing tools.

2. Ask a friend to bury a container or bottle of water in the ground (don't forget to first ask for permission to dig).

3. Now try to find the water by holding the forked ends of the dowsing stick with the stem pointing straight ahead. Walk very slowly across the area where you think that the water is hidden.

4. Concentrate on finding the water as you walk.

5. If the stick points down or twitches, ask your friend if you have found the correct spot, then dig.

6. You may need to give it several tries—it takes time to learn a new skill!

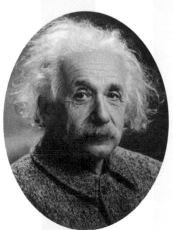

I know very well that many scientists consider dowsing to be a type of ancient superstition. According to my conviction, this is, however, unjustified. The dowsing rod is a simple instrument which shows the reaction of the human nervous system to certain factors which are unknown to us at this time.
—*Albert Einstein, German-born American physicist (1879–1955)*

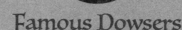

Famous Dowsers

Some well-known people who dabbled in dowsing include
artist **Leonardo da Vinci** and scientists
Sir Isaac Newton, **Thomas Edison**, and Albert Einstein.

Searching for More

Dowsing is also used to find hidden minerals, oil, and gas; missing people and pets; ships lost at sea; and even ghosts! Egypt's Queen Cleopatra used dowsers to search for gold, and England's **Queen Elizabeth I** hired dowsers to help local miners find tin deposits.

When the Sky Is Dry

Vineyards and small farms in California hired dowsers during the 2014 drought. The growers were desperate to find new wells on their properties because the old wells had dried up.

183

AMUSEMENT

Caves Uncovered

In October 2017, friends Luc Le Blanc and David Caron used a wooden dowsing rod to discover a huge Ice Age cave system, formed more than 15,000 years ago, under the city of Montreal, Quebec.

Divine Doodle Witching

Other names for dowsing include divining, doodle-bugging, and water-witching.

Dowsing in History

- An engraving (above) in the 16th-century book *De Re Metallica* shows two men with forked sticks searching for minerals and miners digging them up nearby.

- An 8,000-year-old painting on a wall in a North African cave shows a dowser holding a Y-branch.

- Ancient dowsing tools have been found in Egypt and China.

Dowsing for Treasure

In 1989, dowser Jimmy Longton found a Viking treasure near Penrith, England, worth more than $60,000. Ten years later, he helped to find *The Blessing of Burntisland*, a 17th-century shipwreck off the coast of Scotland. The ship contained valuables belonging to **King Charles I** of England.

DO YOU HAIKU?

Poetry is a creative way of expressing feelings and ideas. Have you ever heard of haiku (hi-KOO) poems? Basho, a master poet in 17th-century Japan, made this form popular. He wrote haikus to record what he saw on his travels. Here's an example:

Even a thatched hut
May change with a new owner
Into a doll's house.

FOLLOW THE RULES

North Americans began writing haiku in the early 1900s. English-language haiku . . .

- has only 17 syllables
- has only three lines
- has five syllables in the first line, seven in the second, and five in the third
- does not rhyme
- is often about nature

For example:
Blue heron watches.
Past his reflection is lunch.
The color of rain.

PUZZLING POEMS

Sometimes haiku can be written like a riddle. Can you guess what this one is about?

Green and thirsty fans
Cheer from the treetops in spring.
Autumn brings them down.

Did you guess leaves? You are right!

HAIKU HOW-TO

- For ideas for haikus, explore something. Go for a walk or a bike ride or look through these pages!
- Did you see a squirrel burying a nut? A tiny weed pushing up? A cat flicking its tail?
- Write a list of words about your topic and follow the rules for writing a haiku.
- Once you get the hang of it, try other topics.

FOUR SEASONS OF HAIKU

Under winter's Sun
Icicles crackle a song
Then shatter below.

Spring morning routine
Robin taps against window
A new alarm clock.

On a summer's breeze
Spiderlings parachute down
Prepare for landing!

Light of autumn Moon
Pours through weeping willow boughs
Like a bowl of cream.

–Brenda Huante

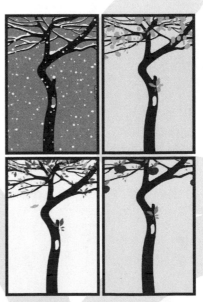

FUN WITH THE SUN

Be a photographer—without a camera.
All you need is the Sun and photosensitive paper.*

YOU WILL NEED:
piece of cardboard, at least 5x7 inches
several sheets of 5x7-inch photosensitive paper
leaves, flowers, paper clips, or other small objects
piece of glass, 5x7 inches
plastic tray or dish, about 8x10 inches
paper towels

1. Place the cardboard on a flat surface. Lay a piece of the photosensitive paper on it, with the white side down.

2. Arrange your objects on top of the paper. Cover them with the piece of glass to hold them in place.

3. Carefully move the cardboard and paper arrangement to a place where it will be in sunshine for at least 8 minutes.

4. While waiting for the picture to develop, fill the tray or dish with water.

5. Carefully bring the cardboard, paper, objects, and glass indoors. Remove the glass and objects and rinse the paper in the tray of water.

6. To dry the print, lay the paper flat on the paper towels.

Look for photosensitive paper at craft and photography stores.

TABLE OF MEASURES

LENGTH/DISTANCE

1 foot = 12 inches
1 yard = 3 feet = 0.914 meter
1 meter = 39.37 inches
1 mile = 1,760 yards = 5,280 feet = 1.61 kilometers
1 kilometer = 0.62 mile

AREA

1 square inch = 6.45 square centimeters
1 square foot = 144 square inches
1 square yard = 9 square feet = 0.84 square meter
1 acre = 43,560 square feet = 0.40 hectare
1 hectare = 2.47 acres
1 square mile = 640 acres = 2.59 square kilometers
1 square kilometer = 0.386 square mile

HOUSEHOLD

(approx. equivalents)
½ teaspoon = 2 mL
1 teaspoon = 5 mL
3 teaspoons = 1 tablespoon = 15 mL
¼ cup = 60 mL
⅓ cup = 75 mL
½ cup = 125 mL
¾ cup = 175 mL
1 cup = 16 tablespoons = 8 ounces = 250 mL
2 liquid cups = 1 pint = 0.5 liter
2 liquid pints = 1 quart = 1 liter
4 liquid quarts = 1 gallon = 3.78 liters

SPEED/VELOCITY

(mph = miles per hour;
kph = kilometers per hour)
1 mph = 1.609 kph
1 knot = 1.15 mph = 1.85 kph

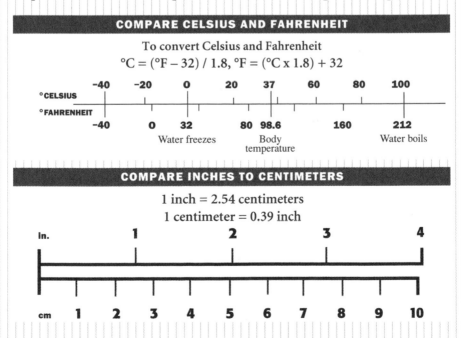

COMPARE CELSIUS AND FAHRENHEIT

To convert Celsius and Fahrenheit
$$°C = (°F − 32) / 1.8, °F = (°C × 1.8) + 32$$

°CELSIUS	-40	-20	0	20	37	60	80	100
°FAHRENHEIT	-40	0	32	80	98.6		160	212

Water freezes — Body temperature — Water boils

COMPARE INCHES TO CENTIMETERS

1 inch = 2.54 centimeters
1 centimeter = 0.39 inch

in. 1 2 3 4

cm 1 2 3 4 5 6 7 8 9 10

AMUSEMENT

ACKNOWLEDGMENTS

PICTURE CREDITS

ABBREVIATIONS:
GI—Getty Images
NASA—National Aeronautics and
Space Administration
PX—Pixabay
SS—Shutterstock
TS—Thinkstock
WM—Wikimedia

Front cover: (Panda) Rocter/GI.
(Housefly) Backiris/GI. (Uranus) NASA/
SS. (Bald eagle) Andyworks/GI. (Chicken)
memoangles/GI.
Calendar: 8: (Bottom center, top)
Reimphoto/GI. (Bottom center, bottom)
PX. 9: (Top) GBlakeley/GI. (Center)
paci77/GI. (Bottom) St. Louis Zoo. 10:
(Top left) PX. (Center right) PX. 11: (Top
left) Iryna Shkrabaliuk/GI. (Center right)
WM. (Bottom right) 2630ben/GI. (Bottom
left) Takhini Hot Pools. 12: (Top right)
NatureNow/GI. (Center right) PX. 13:
(Top) Maike Hildebrand/GI. (Center left)
bluebearry/GI. (Center right) WM. (Bottom
top) Anna39/GI. (Bottom) Vladone/GI. 14:
(Bottom center, top) 123dartist/GI.
(Bottom center, bottom) Diana Taliun/
GI. 15: (Top) Pinterest. (Center right)
ClaudioVentrella/GI. (Bottom left)
adogslifephoto/GI. (Bottom right)
prmustafe/GI. 16: (Center right)
moussa81/GI. (Bottom right, top)
Mantonature/GI. (Bottom right, bottom)
Igor Krasilov/GI. 17: (Top) WM. (Center)
WM. (Bottom) blueringmedia/GI. 18:
(Bottom right, top) MsLightBox/GI.
(Bottom right, bottom) PX. 19: (Top right)
Charlie Cowins/Flickr/WM. (Center left)
FatCamera/GI. (Center right) brgfx/GI.
(Bottom) MagnoliaReporter.com. 20: (Top
left) mahod84/GI. (Bottom) MollyNZ/
GI. 21: (Top) mrtom-uk/GI. (Center right)
Nymag.com. (Bottom) luamduan/GI.
22: (Bottom left, top) Haluk Köhserli/GI.

(Bottom) PX. 23: (Top) cmannphoto/GI.
(Center left) U.S. Coast Guard. (Bottom
left) OKRAD/GI. (Bottom right) Agência
Brasil Fotografias/WM. 24: (Top right)
Sapphiredge/WM. (Center right) PX. 25:
(Top left) Creative_Outlet/GI. (Top right)
Canadian National Exhibition. (Center
left) WM. (Bottom) spates/GI. 26: (Center
right) dpulitzer/WM. (Bottom, both) PX. 27:
(Top) WM. (Center left) NASA. (Center right)
DigitalStorm/GI. (Bottom) Chokkicx/GI. 28:
(Bottom left, top) PX. (Bottom) TS. 29: (Top)
WM. (Center right) Skathi/GI. (Bottom)
AlexLMX/GI. 30: (Top left) VvoeVale/GI.
(Bottom) TS. 31: (Top left) WM. (Top right)
Alfadanz/GI. (Center left) WM. (Bottom)
VectorStory/GI.
Astronomy: 32–33: NASA/SS. 32:
(Bottom) National Portrait Gallery/WM.
34–35: NASA/SS. 36–39: Tim Robinson.
40–41: Canadian Space Agency. 42–43:
NASA. 44: (Top) Canadian Space Agency.
(Bottom) rossandgaffney/GI. 45: NASA.
46–47: simonbradfield/GI. 48: (Top)
Margarita_Alshina/Instagram. (Bottom)
venusvi/GI. 49: Radoslav Cajkovic/SS. 50:
Bryant Olsen/Flickr. 51: bubu45/GI. 52–
55: Tim Robinson. 56–57: Choreograph/
GI. 58: (Bottom left) Hansonshows.com.
(Bottom right) Drawkman/GI. 59: (Top)
Akiromaru/GI. (Bottom, all) WM. 60:
Alexander Chaikin/SS. 61: (All) PX.
63: Fishbones/GI.
On the Farm: 64–65: asmakar/GI.
64: (Center left) GlobalP/GI. (Center
middle) aluxum/GI. (Center right)
GlobalP/GI. 65: (Top) memoangeles/
GI. (Bottom left) ARTPUPPY/GI. (Bottom
right) Tigatelu/GI. 66–67: asmakar/
GI. 66: (Top) ARTPUPPY/GI. (Center)
Blueringmedia/GI. (Bottom) boric/GI.
67: (Center right) ARTPUPPY/GI. (Bottom
left) Chayapoll Tummakorn/GI. 68–69:
asmakar/GI. 68: (Top) memoangeles/
GI. (Bottom) edopix/GI. 69: (Top) gsagi/
GI. (Center) blueringmedia/GI. (Bottom)

memoangeles/GI. 70: (Background) asmakar/GI. (Center) blueringmedia/ GI. (Bottom) memoangeles/GI. 71: Arinahabich/GI. 72–73: Buffy1982/ SS. 74: (Center) Steven Frame/SS. (Bottom) PioneerMountainHomestead/ SS. 75: (top) OryPhotography/SS. (Center) Sheila Farley/SS. 76: (Top) PioneerMountainHomestead/SS. (Bottom) Buffy1982/SS. 77: (All) Carol Mowdy Bond. 78–81: All photos courtesy of the Albrecht family.
In the Garden: 82–83: Tim Robinson. 84: (Top) TS. (Bottom) juniperberry/ GI. 85: (Left) PicturePartners/ GI. (Right) Natdanai99/SS. 86: (Left) warrengoldswain/GI. (Right) DutchScenery/GI. 87: (All) TS. 88: Heike Rau/SS. 89: (All) leisuretime70/SS. 90: (Left) artpritsadee/SS. (Top) Labrynthe/SS. (Bottom) ErikAgar/GI. 91: (Top left) Kathy Brant/GI. (Top right) HumphreysGarden.com. 92: (Background) arthobbit/GI. (Top) artpritsadee/SS. (Bottom) HumphreysGarden.com. 93: (Top background) saemilee/GI. (Top) Kathy Brant/GI. (Center) Cathy Clark/ SS. (Bottom background) Plateresca/ GI. (Bottom) ArgenLant/GI. 94–95: (Bottom background) Vik_Y/GI. 94: (Top background) Betelgejze/GI. (Top) Amazon. (Bottom left, top) Monrovia. (Bottom left, bottom) Alain Pitault/SS. (Bottom right) skymoon13/GI. 95: (Top background) cokada/GI. (Top) Jerrold James Griffith/ SS. (Bottom left) Anna Gratys/SS. (Bottom right) Labrynthe/SS. 96: (Background) Naddiya/GI. (Top) empire 331/GI. (Center) photolinchin/GI. (Bottom, both) Amazon. 97: (Background) Naddiya/GI. (Top) Bruce Kirchoff/WM. (Bottom) ErikAgar/ GI. 98–99: cgdeaw/SS. 98: (Center) sasimoto/SS. (Bottom) Photology1971/ GI. 99: (Center) dragon_fang/GI. (Bottom) suwan promlang/SS.
Nature: 100: (Top left) Julialine/GI. (Top right) David Callan/GI. (Center) Alaska Icons/GI. (Bottom left) Pavel L Photo and Video/SS. (Bottom right) BrianNRogers/ GI. 101: (Top) Florian Möllers Nature

Picture Library/GI. (Center) roundhill/ GI. 102: roundhill/GI. 103: Robbie Ross/ GI. 104: Fredrik Moe/SS. 105: (Top) Vladimir Filonov/Moscow Times. (Bottom) Pavel L Photo and Video/SS. 106: David Callan/GI. 107: wrangle/GI. 108: Florian Möllers Nature Picture Library/GI. 109: guenterguni/GI. 110: quickshooting/GI. 111: (Top) Erika Parfenova/GI. (Center left) mischach/GI. (Center right) mrdoomits/GI. (Bottom left) tavlphoto/GI. 112: (Top) SondraP/GI. (Top right) hekakoskinen/GI. (Center left) ANGHI/GI. (Bottom right) Ian_Redding/GI. 113: (Top) TT/GI. (Center right) ArchyEmily/GI. (Center left) DavorLovincic/GI. 114–115: Andyworks/GI. 116: (Top) Brian E Kushner/GI. (African eagle) Invisiblewl/GI. (Golden eagle) ian600f/GI. (Harpy eagle) ChepeNicoli/GI. (Javan hawk-eagle) DikkyOesin/GI. 117: (Top right) sqback/GI. (Center left) jocrebbin/GI. (Bottom) Kandfoto/GI. 118: Dssimages/ GI. 119: (All) BirdImages/GI. 120: (Top) avstraliavasin/GI. (Bottom left) Ryan Brohm/GI. (Bottom right) Ivan Marjanovic/ GI. 121: (All) Leonid Eremeychuk/GI. 122: (All) Ivan Marjanovic/GI. 123: egiss/GI.
Awesome Achievers: 124: Haile Thomas/ Facebook. 125: (Background) gibiati/GI. 126: (Background) gibiati/GI. (Top left and right) Liam's Lunches of Love/Facebook. 127: (Background) gibiati/GI. (Bottom) Andy King/Discovery Education 3M Young Scientist Challenge. 128: (Background) gibiati/GI. (Bottom) Cbc.ca. 129: (Background) gibiati/GI. (Top left) Kasey Meredith/Bakersfield.com. (Top right) ClearTheShelters.com. 130: Historic Times. 131: (Top right) JordanRomero .com. (Center right) Twitter. (Bottom) Kickstarter.com.
Food: 132: (Top) Gurzzza/GI. (Bottom) ajaykampani/GI. 133: (Top) anilakkus/GI. (Bottom) pulmarcini/GI. 134: onlyyouqj/GI. 135: (Bottom left) ithinksky/GI. (Bottom right) antpkr/GI. 136: (Top) Watcha/GI. (Bottom) repinanatoly/GI. 137: (Top) Sundry Photography/SS. (Center right) studiovin/SS. 138–139: (Bottom)

AndreaAstes/GI. 138: (Top) GOLFX/GI.
139: (Top) Almanac.com. 140–141:
(Background) Angel_1978/GI. 140:
(Center) Nataniil/GI. (Bottom left)
peliustok/GI. (Bottom right) BoxerX/GI.
141: (Top right and center left) kostins/GI.
(Center right) Allevinatis/GI. (Bottom
left) SergeyZavalnyuk/GI. (Bottom right)
len_pri/GI. 142–143: (Background)
Angel_1978/GI. 142: aoshlick/GI.
143: (All) aoshlick/GI. 144: ahavelaar/GI.
145: (Background) tumoxasan/GI. (Top)
Teen00000/GI. 146–147: (Background)
tumoxasan/GI. 146: LauriPatterson/GI.
147: photosarahjackson/SS.
Sports: 148–151: Tim Robinson.
152–153: Herbert Kratky/SS.
153: (Bottom) Jason_V/GI. 154–155:
(Background) bortonia/GI. 154: (Top)
wfnc_educ/GI. (Center) gbrundin/GI.
155: (Top) Herbert Kratky/SS. (Center)
SimplyCreativePhotography/GI. 156–157:
AdrianHillman/GI.
History: 158: (Background) GI. (Top left)
exxorian/GI. (Center right) PX. (Bottom
left) Vaniatos/GI. 159: GI. 160–161:
(Background) GI. 160: (Top) amnarj2006/
GI. (Center) skodonnell/GI. (Bottom)
PikePlaceMarket.org. 161: Juxtapost.com.
162–163: SmartStock/GI.
Health: 164: Dimitris66/GI. 165: Tera
Vector/GI. 166: (Top) StHelena/GI. (Center)
art4stock/GI. (Bottom) IvanNikulin/GI.
167: (Top) dromp/GI. (Center) annamori/
GI. 168–171: Tim Robinson.
Pets: 172–173: ablokhin/GI. 174: (Top)
Andriy Blokhin/SS. (Bottom) ablokhin/GI.
175: ablokhin/GI. 176–177: Kerrick/GI.
178: GOLFX/GI. 179: olgagorovenko/GI.
Amusement: 180: WikiHow. 181: WM.
182: (Top, all) WM. (Center left)
repinanatoly/GI. (Bottom right) WM. 183:
(Top right) WM. (Center left) Luc Le Blanc.
(Bottom) WM. 184: (Top) WM.
(Bottom) John James Audubon. 185: (Top)
Stefan Grau/GI. (Center) Krimzoya/GI.
(Bottom) paseven/GI.
186: (Background) Zikatuha/SS. (Center)
Andriu_s/GI.

CONTRIBUTORS

Quinten Albrecht: A Farmer's Life for
Me! **Carol Mowdy Bond:** Delightful Dwarf
Goats. **Christopher Burnett:** Irritating
Invertebrates. **Jack Burnett:** Ready, Set,
Success! **Alice Cary:** Let It Snow!, When
Wild Animals Come to Town, Uncommon
Kids. **Melissa Caughey:** Scrambled Facts
About Chickens, excerpted from *How to
Speak Chicken,* used with permission
from Storey Publishing. **Tim Clark:** Journey
Through the Center of Earth, Let the
Games Begin!, Fishing for Fun.
Stephanie Gibeault: Cat Trick Secrets.
Brenda Huante: Four Seasons of Haiku.
Mare-Anne Jarvela: Where Do We Get
Our Food?, The Hows of the Dowse.
Benjamin Kilbride: Dairy Good Recipes.
Barbara Lassonde: Out-of-This-World
Gardening, How the Pig Became a Bank,
Things to Know About Having to Go.
Sheryl Normandeau: Mosses and
Liverworts and Lichens—Oh, My!
Sarah Perreault: Weather Mysteries
Solved!, Grow a First Aid Kit, Sow-Easy
Seed Balls, In a Pickle, Curlers Are Cool!,
The Eyes Have It, Pet-iculars.
Stephanie Shaw: Do You Haiku?
Janice Stillman: Calendar, Weather
Mysteries Solved!, Adrift on the Ice, The
Ups and Downs of Vegetables, Nature's
Party Plants, Revolutionary Minutes.
Heidi Stonehill: Uranus: Planet of
Surprises, Our Regal Eagle.

Content not cited here is adapted from
The Old Farmer's Almanac archives or
appears in the public domain. Every
effort has been made to attribute all
material correctly. If any errors have
been unwittingly committed, they will be
corrected in a future edition.

INDEX

ACTIVITIES